Quick Classroom Skits

by Robin Pranga and Cynthia Payne

illustrated by Chris Nye

Eight thematic musical programs for
kindergarten and first grade classes, complete
with ideas for presentation and patterns for
hats and character bibs.

Fearon Teacher Aids
A Division of Frank Schaffer Publications, Inc.

Senior Editor: Kristin Eclov
Editor: Cindy Barden
Copyeditor: Christine Hood
Interior Design: Good Neighbor Press, Inc., Grand Junction, CO
Cover Illustration: Nancee McClure
Illustration: Chris Nye

Fearon Teacher Aids products were formerly manufactured and distributed by American Teaching Aids, Inc., a subsidiary of Silver Burdett Ginn, and are now manufactured and distributed by Frank Schaffer Publications, Inc. FEARON, FEARON TEACHER AIDS, and the FEARON balloon logo are marks used under license from Simon & Schuster, Inc.

© **Fearon Teacher Aids**
A Division of Frank Schaffer Publications, Inc.
23740 Hawthorne Boulevard
Torrance, CA 90505-5927

FE7957
ISBN 1-56417-972-9

Table of Contents

Introduction

Quick Classroom Skits was developed as a resource for kindergarten and first grade teachers. This collection of eight musical skits require minimal preparation by the teacher. The musicals are theme-based and written to familiar tunes that children love to sing. If you are not familiar with any of the melodies, you will find most of the music in the following resources:

- *Do Your Ears Hang Low?* by Tom Glazer. (Doubleday, 1980).

- *Eye Winker Tom Tinker Chin Chopper* by Tom Glazer. (Doubleday, 1973).

- *The Fireside Book of Children's Songs* by Marie Winn. (Simon & Schuster, 1966).

- *Go In and Out the Window* by Dan Fox. (Henry Holt, 1987).

- *How Much Is That Doggie In the Window?* by Bob Merrill. (Whispering Coyote Press, 1997).

- *Jane Yolen's Mother Goose Songbook* by Jane Yolen. (Caroline House, 1992).

- *Music and You.* (Macmillan, 1988).

- *Songs We Sing from Rodgers and Hammerstein.* (Simon & Schuster, 1957).

- *Treasury of Folk Songs* by Tom Glazer. (Grosset & Dunlap, 1964).

Suggestions for scenery and ideas for presentation of the programs help make class musicals easier. With simple modifications, these programs could be performed by individuals or large groups. Patterns for simple costumes that children can help make are also included.

We Can Sing a Rainbow

Scenery

Draw a rainbow on bulletin-board paper. Have students fill in the sections with their handprints using the colors of the rainbow—red, orange, yellow, green, blue, and purple. Hang the rainbow on the wall and use it as a backdrop.

Costumes

1. Have students dress in T-shirts or clothing to represent the colors of the rainbow.

2. Make rainbow hats. (See pattern on page 7.)

Presentation

Divide the class into six groups. Assign a color to each group. Have groups sit in six locations across the stage or classroom or arrange in a rainbow formation. (Red in the back row, orange next, then yellow, and so forth.) All groups sing opening and closing songs. Individual groups sing their assigned songs at the appropriate time.

Related Books To Share With Your Class:

Babar's Book of Color by Laurent De Brunhoff. (Random, 1984).

Brown Bear, Brown Bear, What Do You See? by Bill Martin, Jr. (Holt, 1983).

Color is Everywhere by Cindy Barden. (Judy/Instructo, 1995).

Colors to Know by Karen Gundersheimer. (Harper, 1986).

Colors to Talk About by Leo Lionni. (Pantheon, 1985).

Green Eggs and Ham by Dr. Seuss. (Random House, 1960).

Hailstones and Halibut Bones by Mary O'Neill. (Doubleday, 1973).

Of Colors and Things by Tana Hoban. (Greenwillow, 1986).

Peter Rabbit's Colors by Beatrix Potter. (Viking, 1988).

What Color? A Rainbow Zoo by Fiona Pragoff. (Doubleday, 1987).

Who Said Red? by Mary Serfozo. (Macmillan, 1985).

1

Opening Song

The Rainbow Song
(Sung to the tune "Bingo")

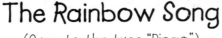
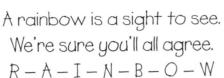

A rainbow is a sight to see.
We're sure you'll all agree.
R – A – I – N – B – O – W
Yes sir-ee
A rainbow is a sight to see.
Of that you can be sure of!

Red, orange, yellow, green, and blue,
And last of all there's purple.
R – A – I – N – B – O – W
Yes sir-ee
A rainbow is a sight to see.
Of that you can be sure of!

Group 1:

Red
(Sung to the tune "Yankee Doodle")

You'll find red most anywhere,
Inside the house or out.
It's our favorite you can see,
For that there is no doubt!

Red's the color we like best,
Red's our favorite color.
Red's the color we like best,
To us there is no other.

Group 2:

Orange
(Sung to the tune "Three Blind Mice")

We like orange. We like orange.
Do you like it too? Do you like it too?
Orange is the color of carrots and juice,
Our Halloween pumpkin, the beak on a goose.
Have you ever seen such a color my friend as,
Orange, orange, orange.

Song 3:

Yellow
(Sung to the tune "Oh, What a Beautiful Morning")

Oh what a beautiful morning,
Oh what a beautiful day.
Without the color of yellow,
There would be no bright sunny days.

I like to eat ripe bananas.
I like to smell daffodils.
Yellow's my favorite color.
It really gives me a thrill!

Group 4:

Green
(Sung to the tune "My Bonnie Lies Over the Ocean")

Green is our favorite color.
The color of grass and the trees.
When we look out our window,
Green is the color we see.

Green, green, green, green,
You are the color we love the best.
Green, green, green, green,
You're better than all of the rest.

Group 5:

Blue
(Sung to the tune "Up on the Housetop")

Down by the ocean we like to play,
In the blue water everyday.
When there are rain clouds in the sky,
We hope they soon will pass us by.

Blue, blue, blue, we love you!
Blue, blue blue, we love you!
You brighten up a rainy day.
Blue, never, never go away!

Reproducible

Group 6:

"Purple"
(Sung to the tune "Teddy Bear's Picnic")

Purple's a color we like a lot.
We thing that it's really grand.
You see it on raisins and grapes and plums,
And flowers all over the land.

We like it best because it's so bright.
We like it best both morning and night.
We sing this song cause purple's our favorite color.

Closing Song:

"The Rainbow Song"
(Sung to the tune "Bingo")

We hope you like to hear us sing,
The colors of the rainbow,
R – A – I – N – B – O – W
Yes sir-ee,
A rainbow is a sight to see.
Of that you can be sure of!

Directions for Hats:

Cut two 2" x 12" (5cm x 30cm) pieces of construction paper and fit to the students' heads. Copy the rainbow and cloud patterns (page 7) on white construction paper. A paper plate cut in half can also be used for the rainbow.

Have students color the sections in the following order from top to bottom: *red, orange, yellow, green, blue,* and *purple.* Cut out the cloud pattern. Paint with diluted glue solution and cover with cotton. Glue the cloud to one end of the rainbow. With glue or staples, attach "rainbow" to the headband.

<u>Alternate:</u> Instead of attaching cotton, write the students' names on the clouds.

Patterns for Rainbow Hat

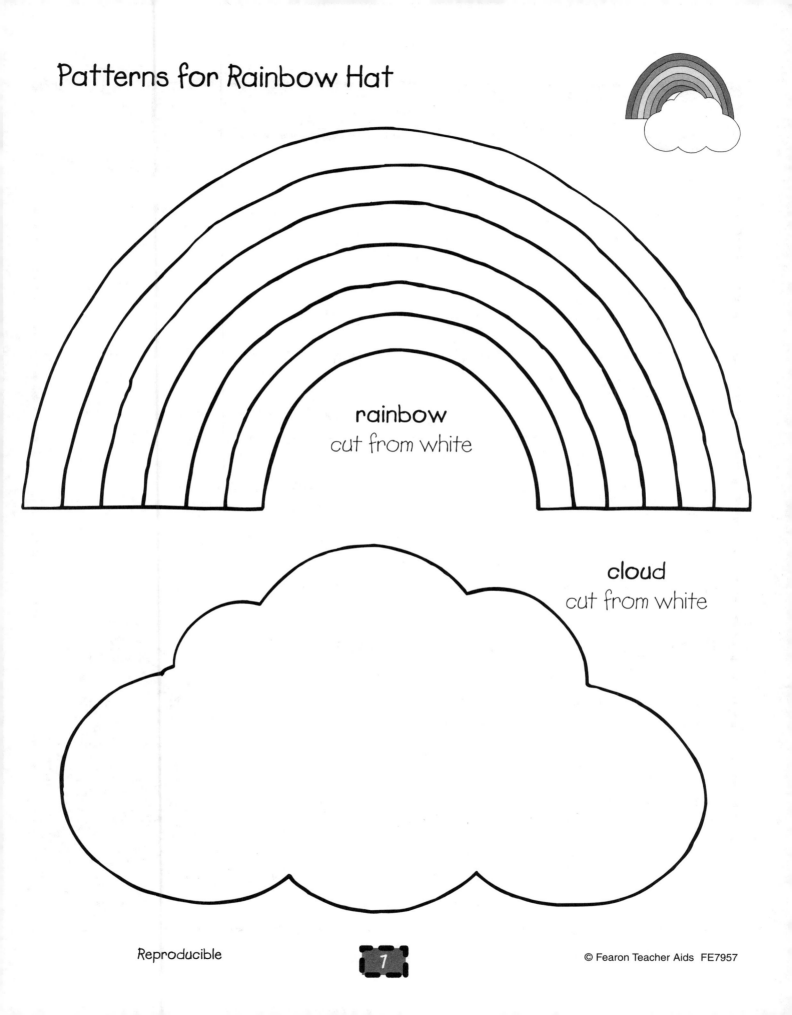

rainbow
cut from white

cloud
cut from white

Grandpa's Farm

Scenery

Paint a farm mural on bulletin-board paper. Suggestions for items to include on the mural are a barn, a pond, a fence, a cornfield, etc. Optional items to enhance the set are cornstalks, bales of hay and farm equipment.

Costumes

1. Have students dress in plaid shirts, blue jeans and kerchiefs.

2. Make animal character bibs and farmer hats. (See patterns on pages 15 to 31.)

Presentation

The class as a whole can sing the songs while individual students or groups of students are designated as the individual animals. As the class sings about an animal, those children representing that animal come forward and perform animal actions to the side or in front of the group. Students in the group not assigned an animal part can wear farmer hats.

The class can also be divided into six groups. Assign an animal to each group. All individuals in the group will wear the animal bib for that animal. Groups sit in separate locations across the stage. Everyone sings the opening and ending songs. The individual groups sing the songs for their designated animals.

Related Books To Share With Your Class:

Animals on the Farm by Feodor Rojankovsky. (Knopf, 1967).
Big Red Barn by Margaret Wise Brown. (Harper, 1989).
Cock-a-Doodle-Doo by Franz Brandenberg. (Greenwillow, 1986).
Farm Animals by Phoebe Dunn. (Random, 1984).
Is Anyone Home? by Ron Maris. (Greenwillow, 1986).
Spots, Feathers, and Curly Tails by Nancy Tafuri. (Greenwillow, 1988).
The Big Sneeze by Ruth Brown. (Lothrop, 1985).
The Day Jimmy's Boa Ate the Wash by Trinka Hakes Noble. (Dial, 1980).
The Wonderful Hay Tumble by Kathleen Harris. (Morrow, 1988).
This Farm is a Mess by Leslie McGuire. (Parents, 1981).

Opening Song:

Grandpa's Farm
(Sung to the tune "Yankee Doodle")

I like to go to grandpa's farm.
There's always lots to do.
The animals are fun to watch,
Would you like to come, too?

Pigs and cows and chicks and hens,
Would you like to see them?
There's a lot to see and do.
The fun is never ending.

Group 1:

The Pig
(Sung to the tune "A Little White Duck")

There's a little pink pig rolling in the mud,
A little pink pig rolling in the mud.
He eats and eats and he gets real fat.

He's the bacon for your breakfast,
Just imagine that!
There's a little pink pig rolling in the mud.
Oink, oink, oink!

Group 2:

The Sheep
(Sung to the tune "A Little White Duck")

There's a little white sheep grazing in the meadow,
A little white sheep grazing in the meadow.
He'll grow a thick, wooly coat of white.
For a blanket to cover me up at night.
There's a little white sheep grazing in the meadow.
Baa, baa, baa.

Group 3:

The Cow
(Sung to the tune "A Little White Duck")

There's a little brown cow grazing in the pasture,
A little brown cow grazing in the pasture.
She eats the grass and she swishes her tail,
And soon she'll give milk that will fill our pail.
There's a little brown cow grazing in the pasture.
Moo, moo, moo.

Group 4:

The Hen
(Sung to the tune "A Little White Duck")

There's a little white hen pecking at the ground,
A little white hen pecking at the ground.
She'll sit and sit on her nest all day.
And that's where she'll lay you a nice big egg.
There's a little white hen pecking at the ground.
Bawk, bawk, bawk.

Reproducible

The Horse

Group 5:

(*Sung to the tune "A Little White Duck"*)

There's a black and white horse,
Running in the meadow,
A black and white horse running in the meadow.
I climb on his back and I take a ride.
When it's time to go in, down his neck I'll slide.
There's a black and white horse,
Running in the meadow.
Nay, nay, nay.

The Dog

Group 6:

(*Sung to the tune "A Little White Duck"*)

There's an old yellow dog sleeping on the porch,
An old yellow dog sleeping on the porch.
He's all worn out because he works all day
Except when I call him to come and play.
There's an old yellow dog sleeping on the porch.
Z-Z-Z-Z-Z, Z-Z-Z-Z-Z, Z-Z-Z-Z-Z.

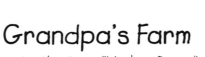

Closing Song:

Grandpa's Farm
(Sung to the tune "Yankee Doodle")

Now that you've been to grandpa's farm,
Hope you've enjoyed the show.
Thanks for your time. We think you're grand.
And now it's time to go.

Pigs and cows and chicks and hens,
You've heard all about them.
Hope you liked the show tonight
Because this is the end!

Directions for Animal Character Bibs

Make character bibs using the following patterns. When completed, punch a hole on each side of the bib, near the top. Attach strings, yarn or ribbons so students can wear the character bibs around their necks.

Pig: Copy patterns from pages 15 to 16 onto construction paper. Glue eyes onto face. Glue ears to top of head. Glue nostrils onto nose. Cut a 1" x 3" (2.5cm x 7.5cm) rectangle from scraps. Glue ends together to form a loop. Glue loop to face and attach nose to the loop. Glue husk to corncob. Glue corncob under the nose.

Reproducible

Sheep: Copy patterns from pages 17 to 19 onto construction paper. Glue wool to top of head. Glue black eyes onto white eye background and glue on face. Glue nose on face. Glue pink inner ear to white outer ear and glue ears to side of head. Glue grass to back of mouth area on head.

Cow: Copy patterns from pages 20 to 22 onto construction paper. Glue horns to top of head. Glue brown mane to top of head between horns. Fold back rectangles in half. Fringe eyelashes and glue to head. Glue brown nose and mouth piece to bottom of head. Glue grass piece under the nose and mouth.

Hen: Copy patterns from pages 23 to 24 onto construction paper. Glue comb to top of head and wattle to bottom of head under chin. Glue black eyes to face. Fold yellow diamond and glue bottom half to face to form beak. Glue brown worm into beak.

Horse: Copy patterns from pages 25 to 26 onto construction paper. Fold back rectangles in half. Fringe mane and eyelashes and glue to face. Using a black marker or crayon draw spots on horse. Draw nostrils on tip of nose. Glue leaf to apple. Glue apple under nose.

13

Dog: Copy patterns from pages 27 to 29 onto construction paper. Glue ears to sides of head. Mount black eye circles onto white eye background. Glue eyes to head. Glue black nose to head and use a black marker or crayon to draw the mouth. Glue paws to the top of bone. Cut a 1" x 3" (2.5cm x 7.5cm) rectangle from scraps and glue ends together to form a loop. Glue loop to bottom of head and attach bone to the loop.

Directions for Farmer Hats:

Copy patterns from pages 30 to 31 onto construction paper. Glue band to hat. Fringe feather and tuck under the band. Glue hat to the front of a 2-inch (5cm) band fitted to the student's head.

Pig Patterns

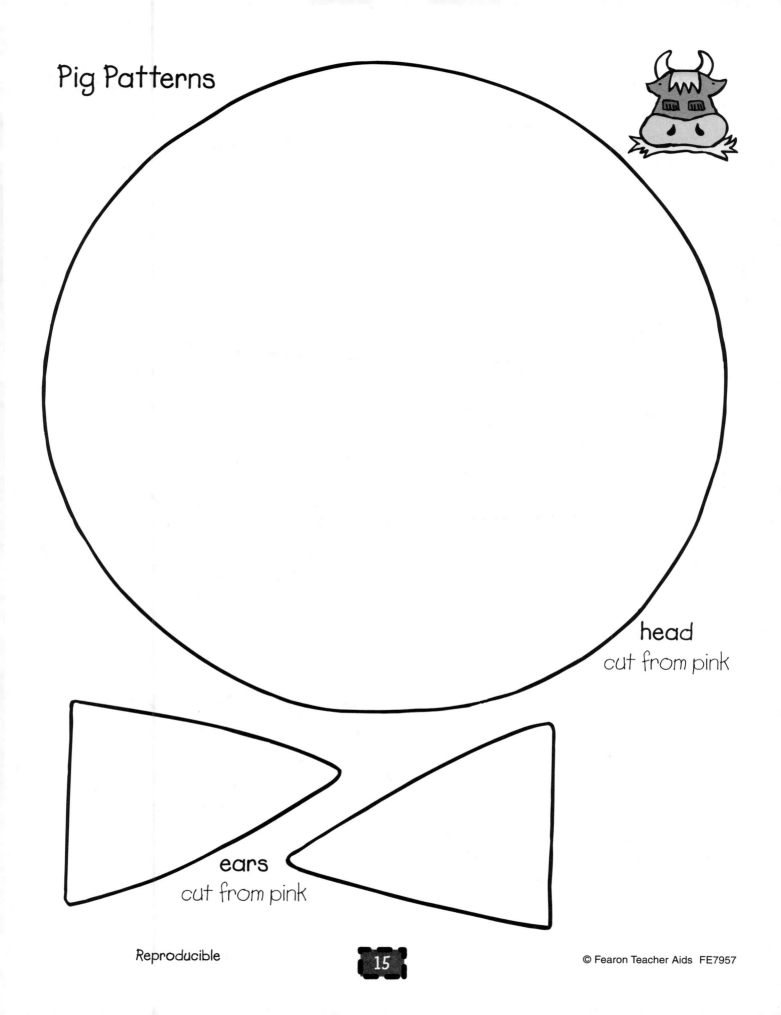

head
cut from pink

ears
cut from pink

Pig Patterns

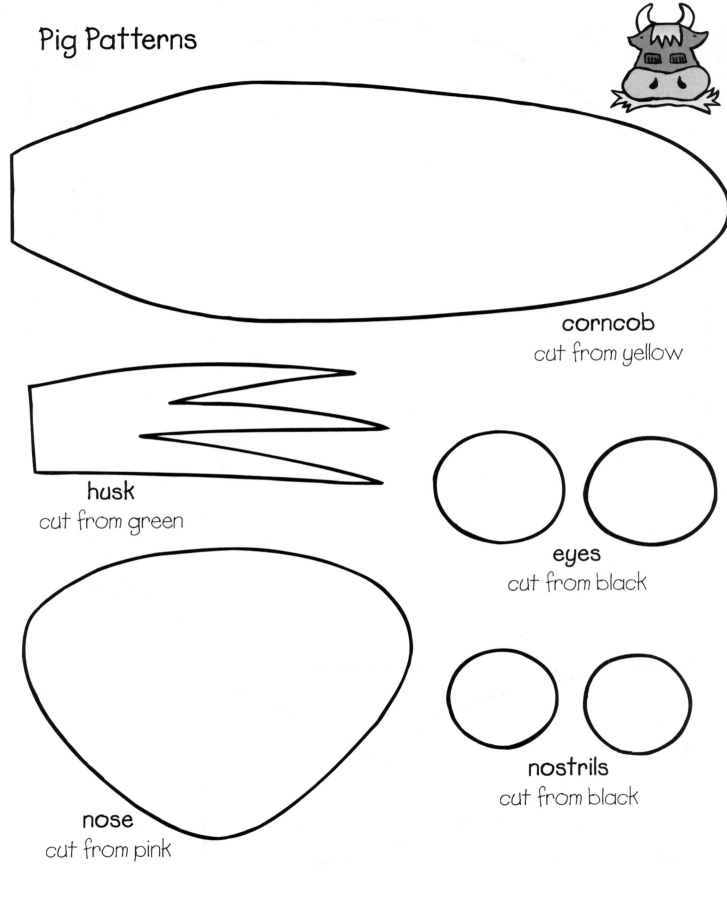

corncob
cut from yellow

husk
cut from green

eyes
cut from black

nose
cut from pink

nostrils
cut from black

Reproducible

Sheep Patterns

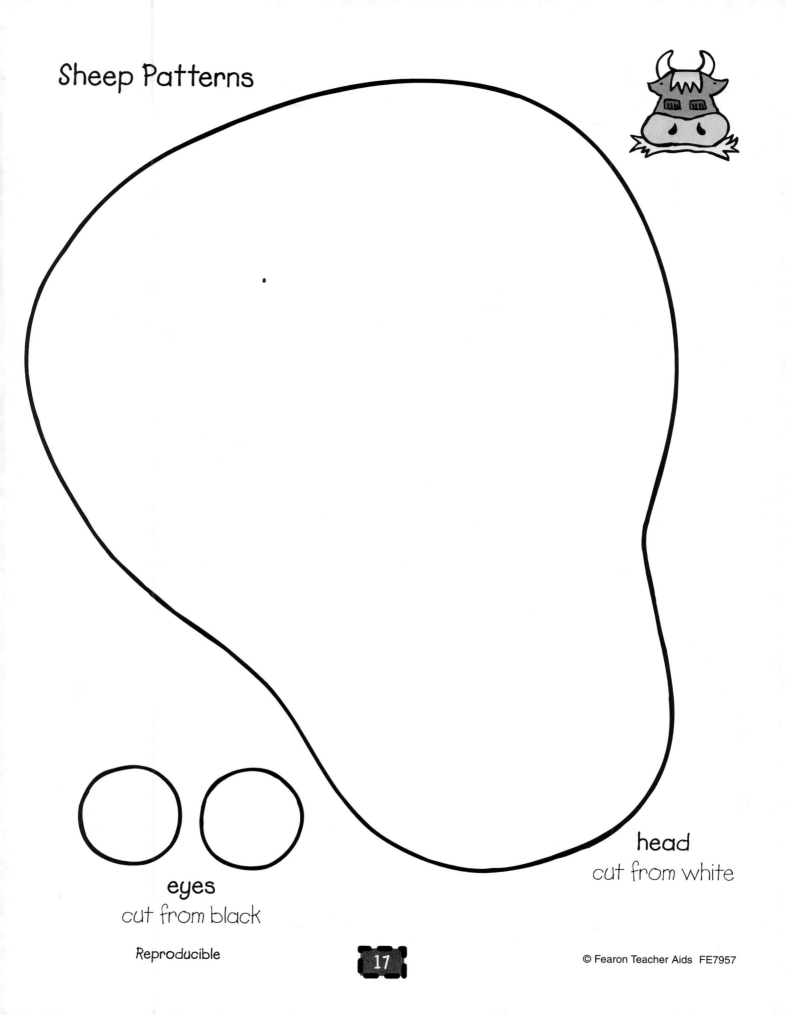

eyes
cut from black

head
cut from white

Sheep Patterns

ears
cut from white

wool
cut from white

18

Reproducible

Sheep Patterns

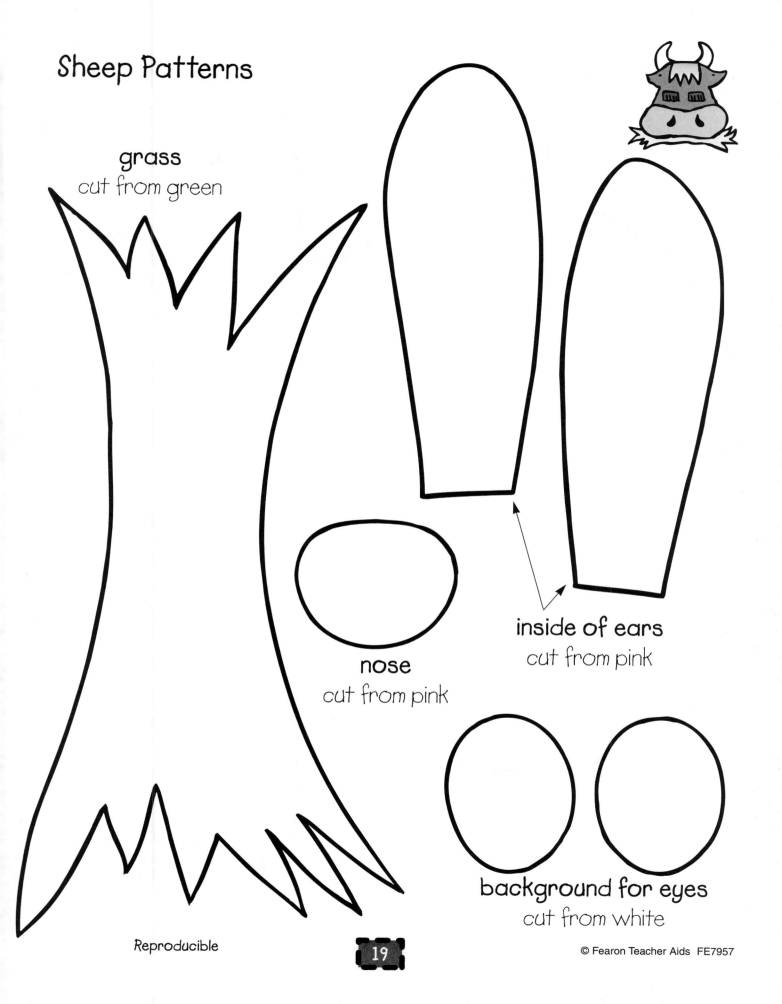

grass
cut from green

nose
cut from pink

inside of ears
cut from pink

background for eyes
cut from white

Cow Pattern

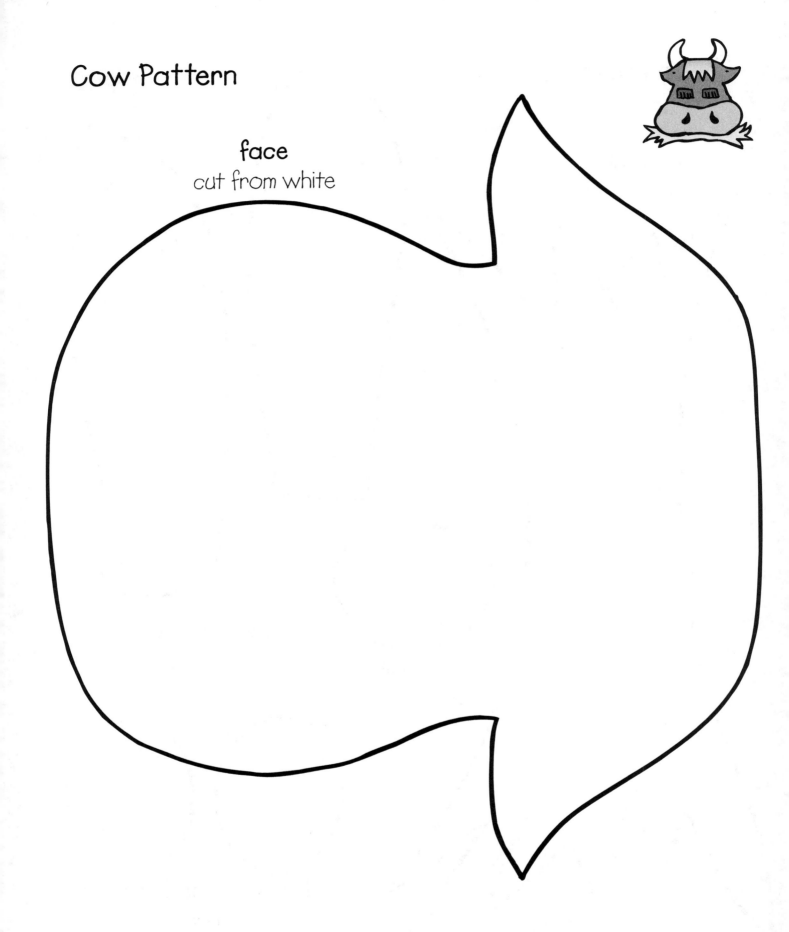

face
cut from white

20

Reproducible

Cow Patterns

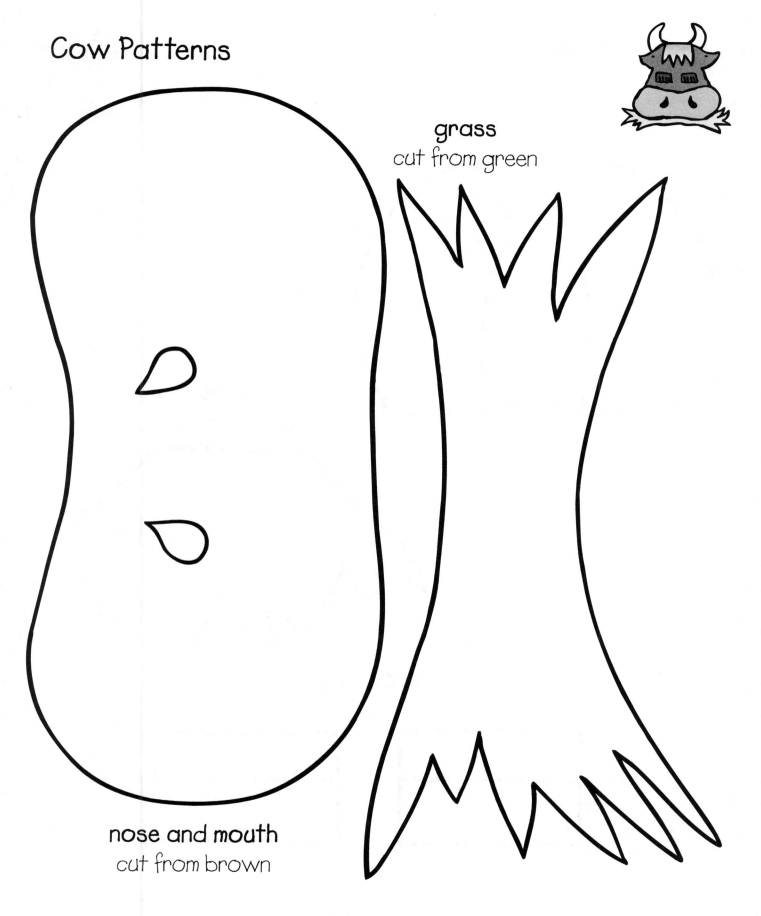

grass
cut from green

nose and mouth
cut from brown

21

© Fearon Teacher Aids FE7957

Cow Patterns

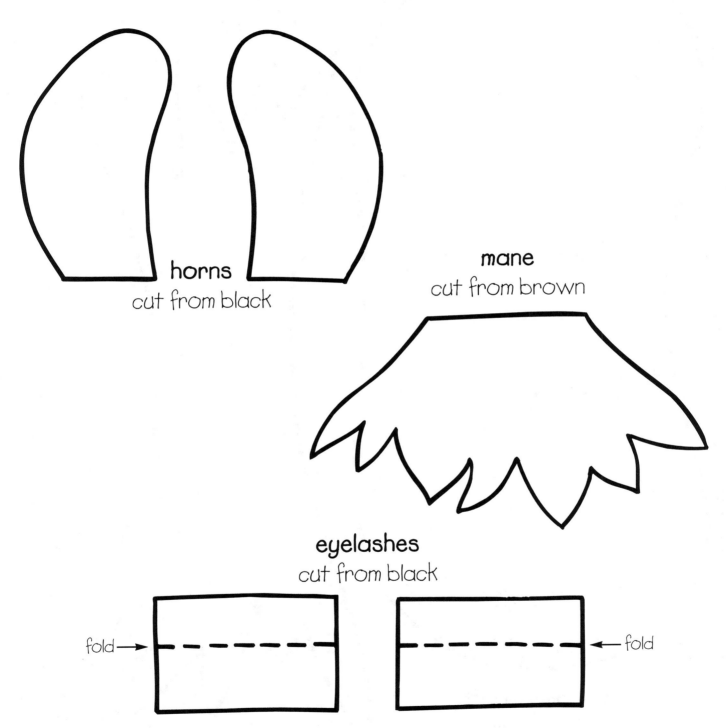

horns
cut from black

mane
cut from brown

eyelashes
cut from black

fold → ← fold

Hen Pattern

head
cut from white

Hen Patterns

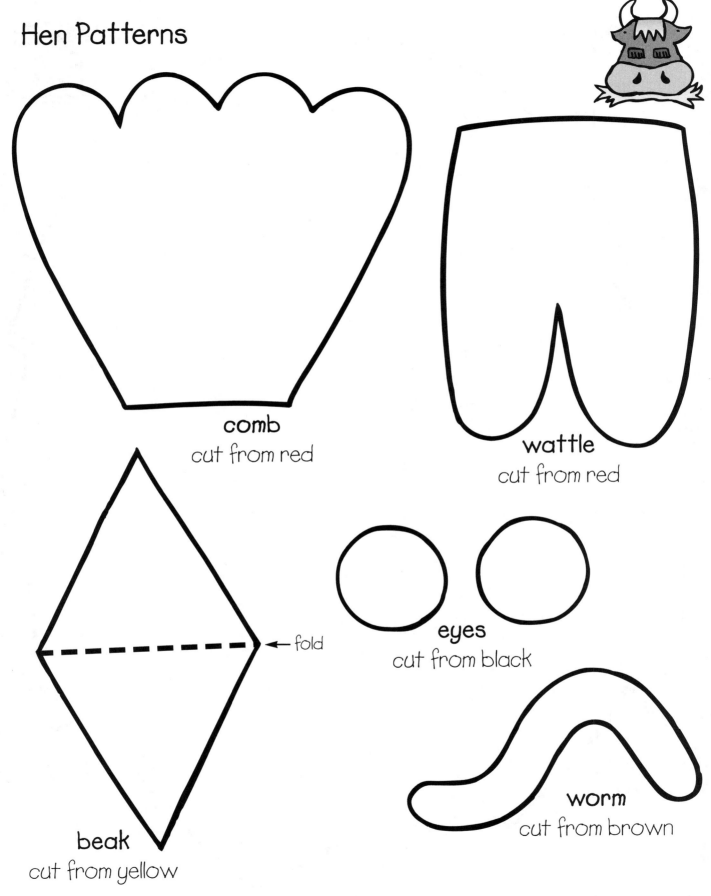

comb

cut from red

wattle

cut from red

← fold

eyes

cut from black

beak

cut from yellow

worm

cut from brown

Reproducible

Horse Pattern

head
cut from white

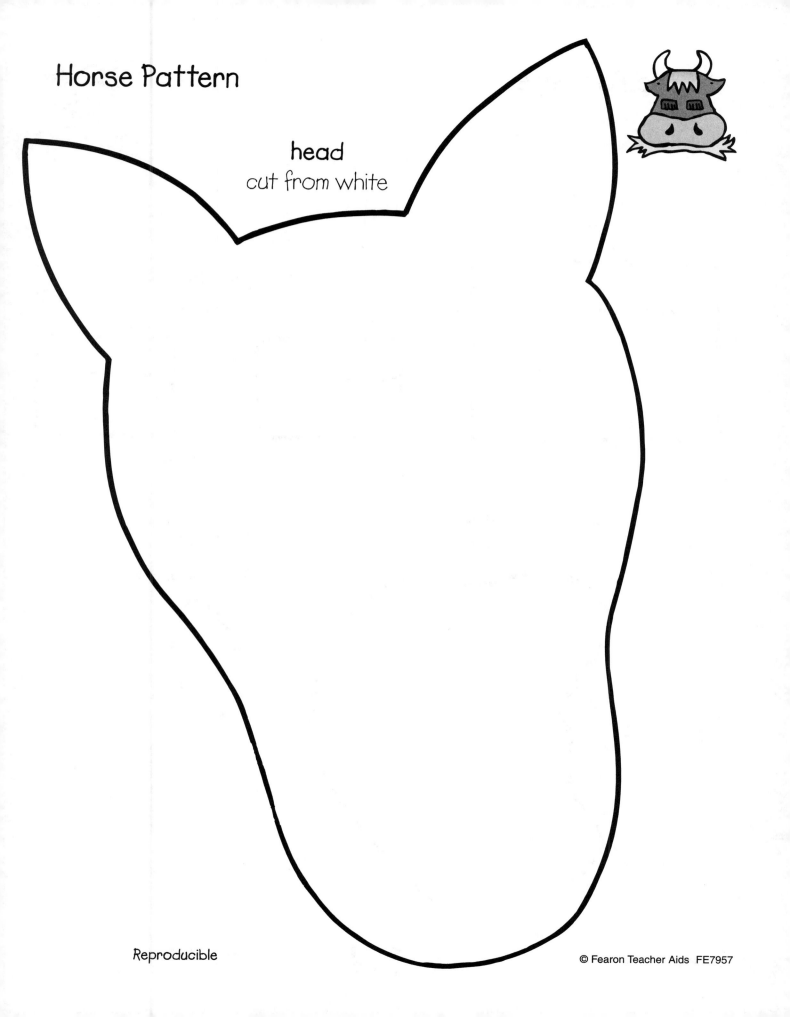

Reproducible

Horse Patterns

mane
cut from black

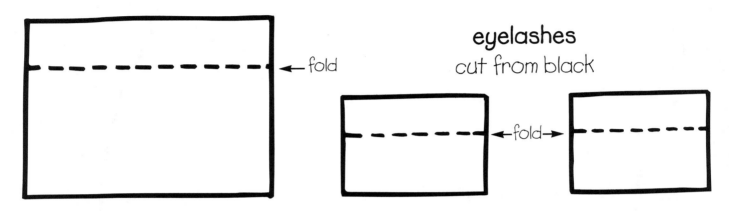

← fold

eyelashes
cut from black

←fold→

apple
cut from red

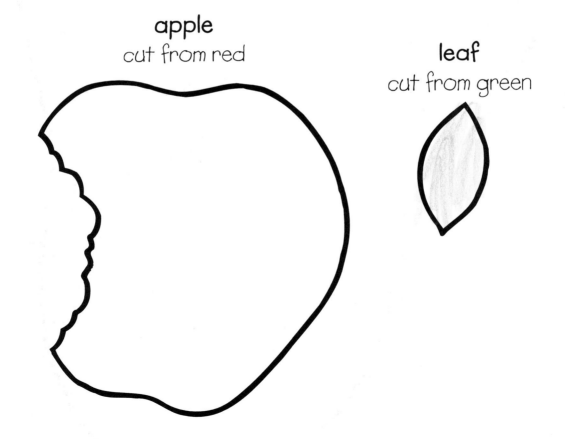

leaf
cut from green

Reproducible

Dog Pattern

head
cut from yellow

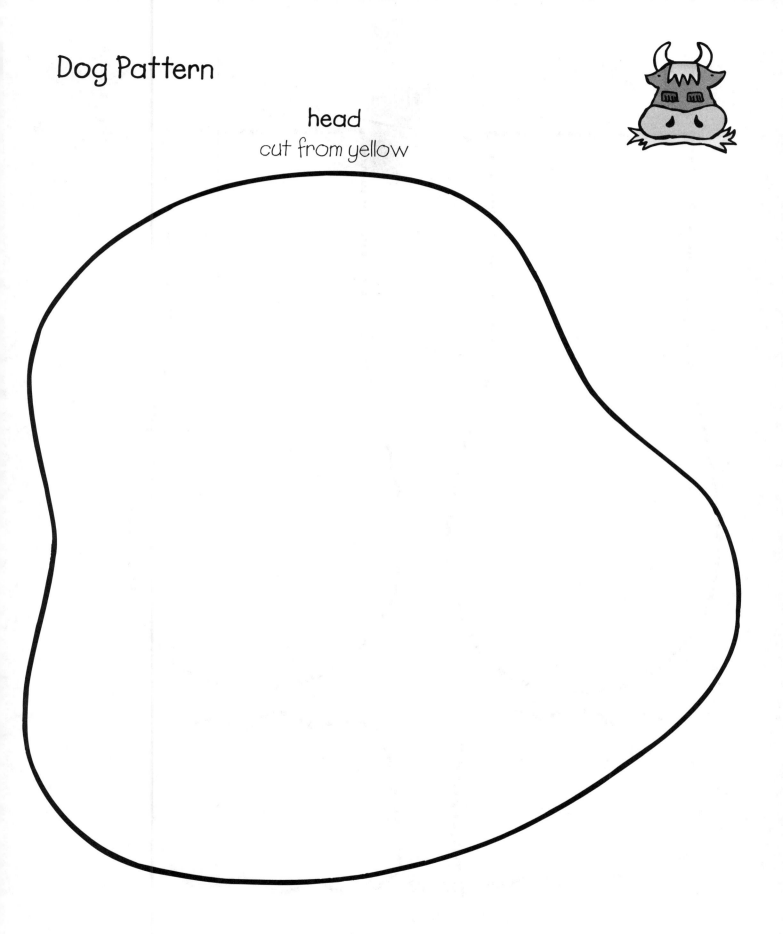

Dog Patterns

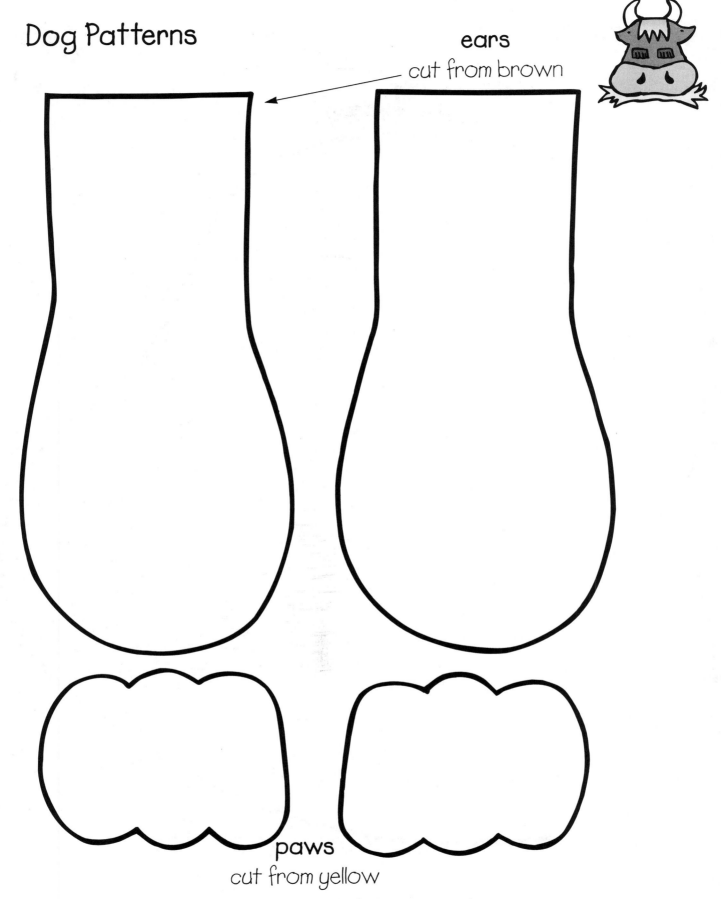

ears
cut from brown

paws
cut from yellow

Dog Patterns

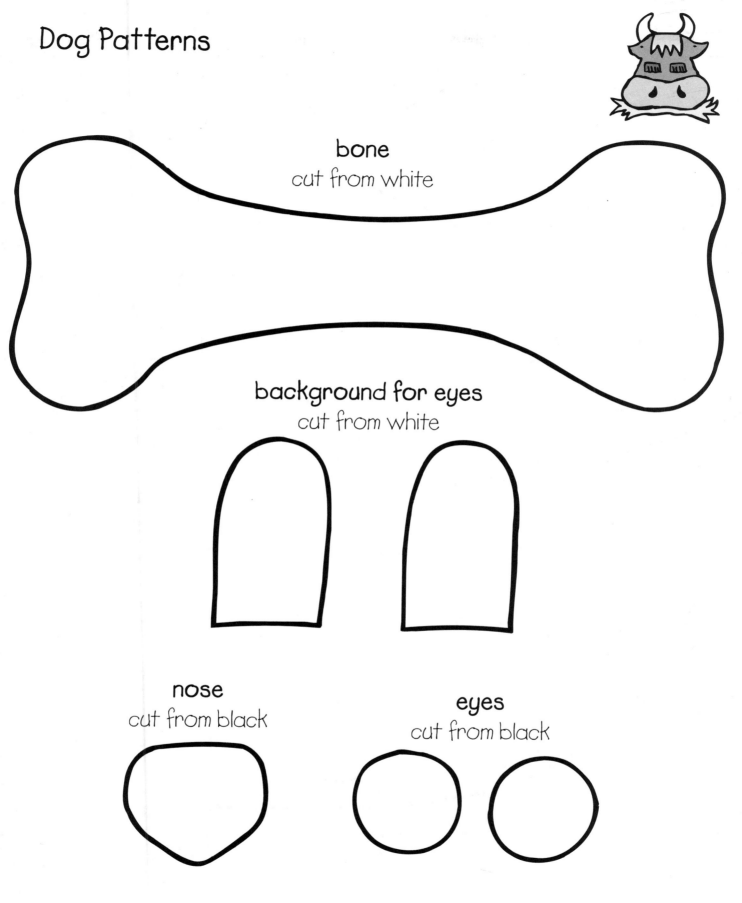

bone
cut from white

background for eyes
cut from white

nose
cut from black

eyes
cut from black

Farmer Hat Pattern

hat
cut from yellow

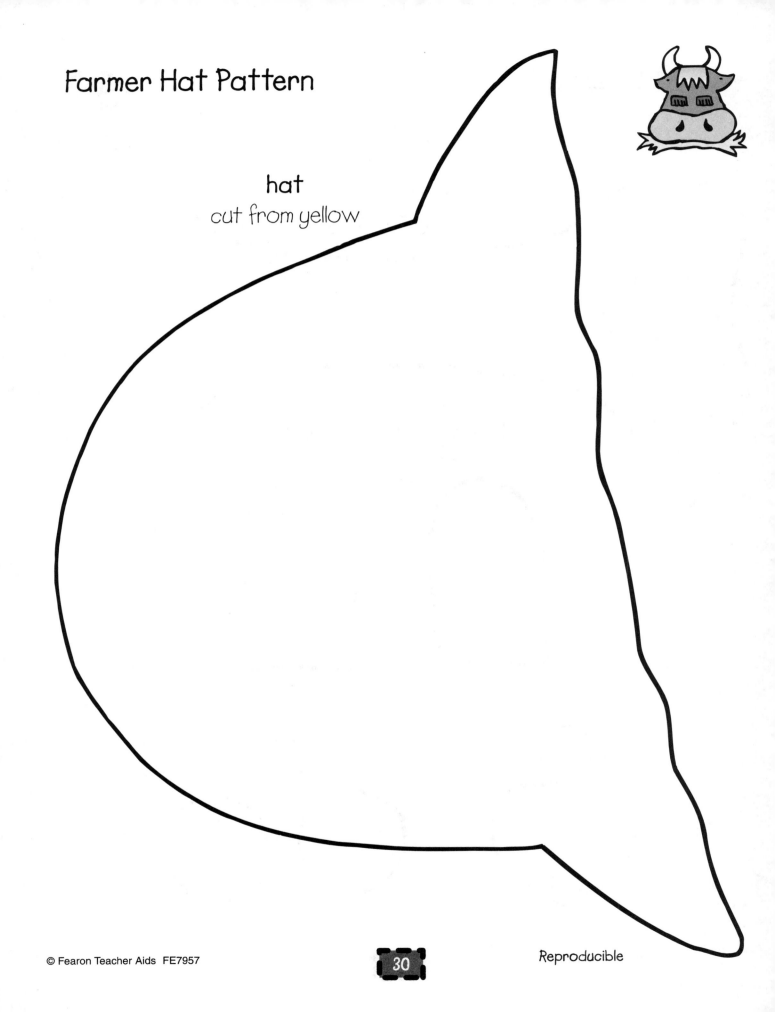

30

Farmer Hat Patterns

hat band
cut from any color

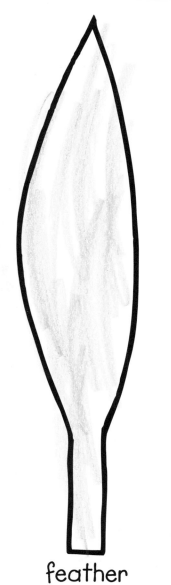

feather
cut from any color

Celebrate the Holidays

Scenery:

Make a mural incorporating symbols from the various holidays included in this section: pumpkins and cornstalks for Halloween, the Mayflower for Thanksgiving, Christmas trees and presents for Christmas, hands of different races joined together to represent peace for Martin Luther King, Jr. Day, hearts for Valentine's Day, and flags and fireworks for Fourth of July.

Costumes:

Halloween: Students wear Halloween costumes.

Thanksgiving: Students dress in black and white and wear Pilgrim hats (see patterns on pages 39 and 42) or dress as Native Americans and wear headdresses. (See pattern on page 41.)

Christmas: Students dress in red and green and wear Santa hats. (See patterns on pages 43 to 44.)

Martin Luther King, Jr. Day: Students wear Martin Luther King, Jr. hats. (See pattern on page 45.)

Valentine's Day: Students dress in red and white and wear Valentine hats. (See pattern on page 46.)

Fourth of July: Students dress in red, white and blue and wear Fourth of July hats or bibs. (See pattern on page 47.)

Presentation:

Divide the class into six groups to represent the six holidays featured in the songs. Each group wears the hat designated for their group. All groups sing the opening and ending songs, while individual groups sing the songs depicting their holidays.

Celebrate the Holidays

Related Books To Share With Your Class:

Halloween:

Arthur's Halloween Costume by Lillian Hoban. (Harper, 1984).

Halloween with Morris and Boris by Bernard Wiseman. (Scholastic, 1986).

Hocus and Pocus at the Circus by Fran Manushkin. (Harper, 1983).

Trick or Treat by Edith Kunhardt. (Greenwillow, 1988).

A Tiger Called Thomas by Charlotte Zolotow. (Lothrop, 1988).

The Witch in the Cherry Tree by Margaret Mahy. (Dent, 1985).

Thanksgiving:

Arthur's Thanksgiving by Marc Brown. (Little, 1983).

Chester Chipmunk's Thanksgiving by Barbara Williams. (Dutton, 1978).

One Terrific Thanksgiving by Marjorie Sharmat. (Holiday, 1985).

Sheriff Sally Gopher and the Thanksgiving Caper by Robert Quackenbush. (Lothrop, 1982).

The Thanksgiving Story by Alice Dalgliesh. (Macmillan, 1988).

Christmas:

Amahl and the Night Visitors by Gian Carlo Menotti. (Morrow, 1986).

Claude the Dog: A Christmas Story by Dick Gackenbach. (Houghton, 1982).

Daniel's Gift by M.C. Helldorfer. (Macmillan, 1987).

Celebrate the Holidays

Petunia's Christmas by Roger Duvoisin. (Knopf, 1952).

Santa's Crash-Bang Christmas by Steven Kroll. (Holiday, 1977).

The Mole Family's Christmas by Russel Hoban. (Scholastic, 1969).

Wake Up, Bear . . . It's Christmas by Stephen Gammel. (Houghton, 1984).

Martin Luther King, Jr. Day:

Martin Luther King Day by Linda Lowery. (Carolrhoda, 1987).

Meet Martin Luther King by James T. De Kay. (Random, 1969).

Valentine's Day:

A Sweetheart for Valentine by Lorna Balian. (Abingdon, 1970).

Bee My Valentine! by Miriam Cohen. (Greenwillow, 1978).

The Best Valentine in the World by Marjorie Sharmat. (Holiday, 1982).

The Valentine's Day Balloon Race by Adrienne Adams. (Macmillan, 1980).

The Valentine's Day Balloon Race by Adrienne Adams. (Macmillan, 1980).

July 4th:

Fourth of July by Charles P. Graves. (Garrand, 1963).

Fourth of July by Barbara M. Josse. (Knopf, 1985).

Henry's Fourth of July by Holly Keller. (Greenwillow, 1985).

The Fourth of July by Mary Kay Phelan. (Harper, 1966).

<u>Opening Song:</u>

Holidays

(Sung to the tune "Ten Little Indians")

Christmas, Thanksgiving, Easter, and Halloween,
New Year's, Valentine's, St. Pat's, and Martin Luther King,
We love the holidays, winter, fall, summer, spring,
Everyday should be a holiday!

Hannukah, Kwanzaa, Mother's Day and Father's Day.
Columbus Day, Labor Day, and Abe Lincoln's birthday,
We love the holidays more than any other days.
Everyday should be a holiday!

<u>Group 1:</u>

Halloween

(Sung to the tune "Teddy Bear's Picnic")

Be careful when you open your door,
If you're alone on Halloween night.
Be careful when you open your door.
Be sure you turn on the light.
For right there standing on your front porch,
Goblins, ghosts, and monsters, all sorts,
Will treat you to a trick if you're out of candy!

Group 2:

Thanksgiving
(Sung to the tune "Hush Little Baby")

Many years ago on a chilly cold day
A ship came sailing into the bay.
Bringing the pilgrims across the sea
To start a new home for you and me.

The Indians met them on this new land,
Working together, hand in hand.
The Pilgrims learned the Indian's ways,
And now we celebrate Thanksgiving Day.

Group 3:

Christmas
(Sung to the tune "Up on the Housetop")

Twinkling lights all around the tree
Lots of presents for you and me!
Turkey and dressing and pumpkin pie,
Grandma and Grandpa by my side.
Christmas is a time for joy.
Christmas is a time for toys.
Family and friends around the tree.
That's what Christmas means to me.

Group 4:

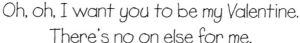

Valentine's Day

(Sung to the tune "Playmate, Come Out and Play With Me")

Oh, oh, I want you to be my Valentine.
There's no on else for me,
But you, oh can't you see,
I'll be the best friend,
That you have ever had?
So be my valentine,
And make me glad.

Group 5:

Martin Luther King Day

(Sung to the tune "Bingo")

There was a man who had a dream,
And Martin was his name-o.
Martin Luther King,
Martin Luther King,
Martin Luther King,
And Martin was his name-o.

He worked for peace across the land,
To bring mankind together.
Martin Luther King,
Martin Luther King,
Martin Luther King,
And Martin was his name-o.

Group 6:

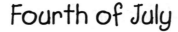

Fourth of July

(Sung to the tune "Yankee Doodle")

Our country has a birthday too.
We celebrate each year.
With picnics and with fireworks,
Red, white and blue we cheer!

Happy Birthday USA,
This day we salute you.
Happy Birthday USA,
With flags red, white and blue.

Closing Song:

Repeat Opening Song

Directions for Hats

For all hats, first construct a two-inch (5cm) band from construction paper to fit students' heads. Use the patterns to make hats for the specific holidays.

Thanksgiving: To make a Native American headdress, cut the headband from yellow, orange or brown. Copy the feather pattern on page 41 onto assorted colors of construction paper. Cut out the number desired, fringe, and attach to the headband. Students may also decorate the headbands with picture writing or geometric shapes.

Thanksgiving—cont'd

To make a pilgrim hat for a girl, use the diagram below. Cut the following pattern from a 12" x 18" (30cm x 45cm) piece of white construction paper. Fold paper along dotted lines. Bend back corners (see diagram) and staple. Punch holes at dots. Attach strings so hat can be tied under chin.

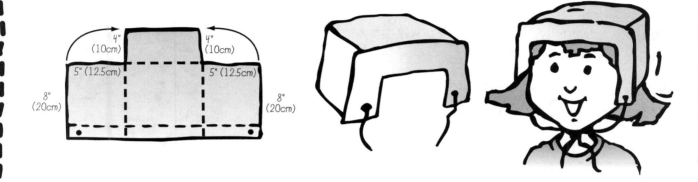

To make a pilgrim hat for a boy, make the headband out of black construction paper. Cut the hat pattern on page 42 from black, the band from white, and glue together. To make the buckle, cut the large square from yellow and the smaller square from white. Glue the white square onto the yellow square. Glue the buckle to the middle of the hatband.

Christmas: Cut headband out of red construction paper. Cut two of each of the Santa hat patterns on pages 43 and 44 from construction paper. Glue two pom poms and two hat bands to red hat sections. If desired, paint pom poms and hat bands with a diluted glue mixture and cover with cotton balls. Glue one hat section to the front of the headband and one section to the back. Glue pom poms together at the top of the hat.

Martin Luther King, Jr. Day: Make hat band out of white construction paper. Using the pattern on page 45, cut out several hands from a variety of skin-tone colors such as pink, brown, tan and yellow. Overlap the hands and glue around the headband.

Valentine's Day: Make hat band out of white construction paper. Using heart patterns on page 46, cut out hearts of various sizes and colors (pink, red, and white) and decorate hat band as desired.

Alternate: Hat bands can be decorated by making patterns of hearts of different colors and sizes. Students may decorate hearts with markers and glitter, etc.

Fourth of July: Make band out of red, white or blue construction paper. Use either the flag or firework pattern on page 47 to color and glue to the front of the hat. If using the flag pattern, attach gummed stars in the corner of the flag. The firework pattern can be decorated with glitter.

Native American Feather Patterns

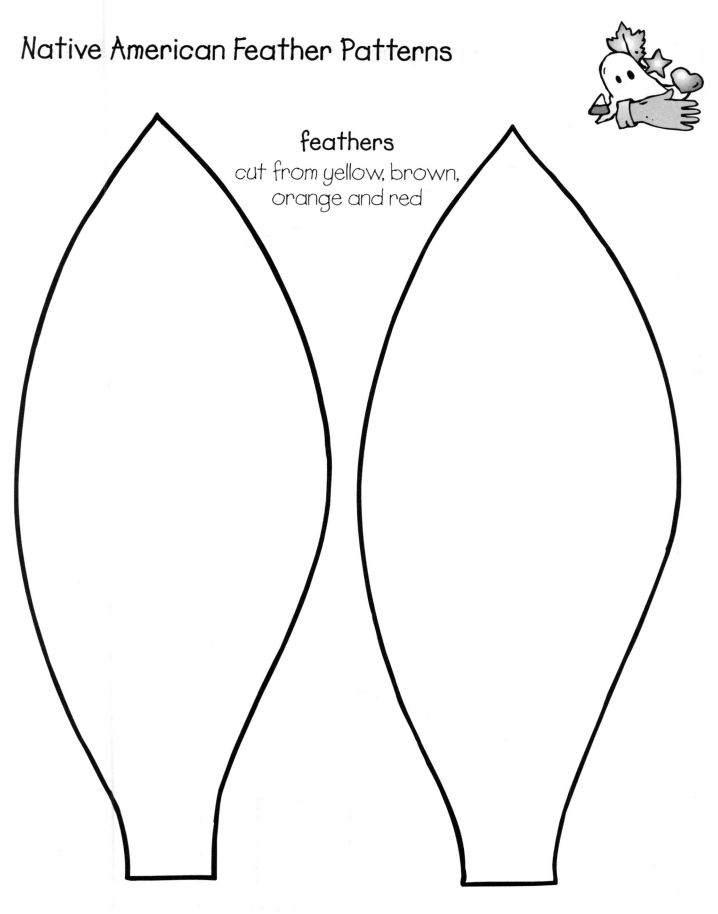

feathers
cut from yellow, brown,
orange and red

Pilgrim Hat Patterns—Boy

hat
cut from black

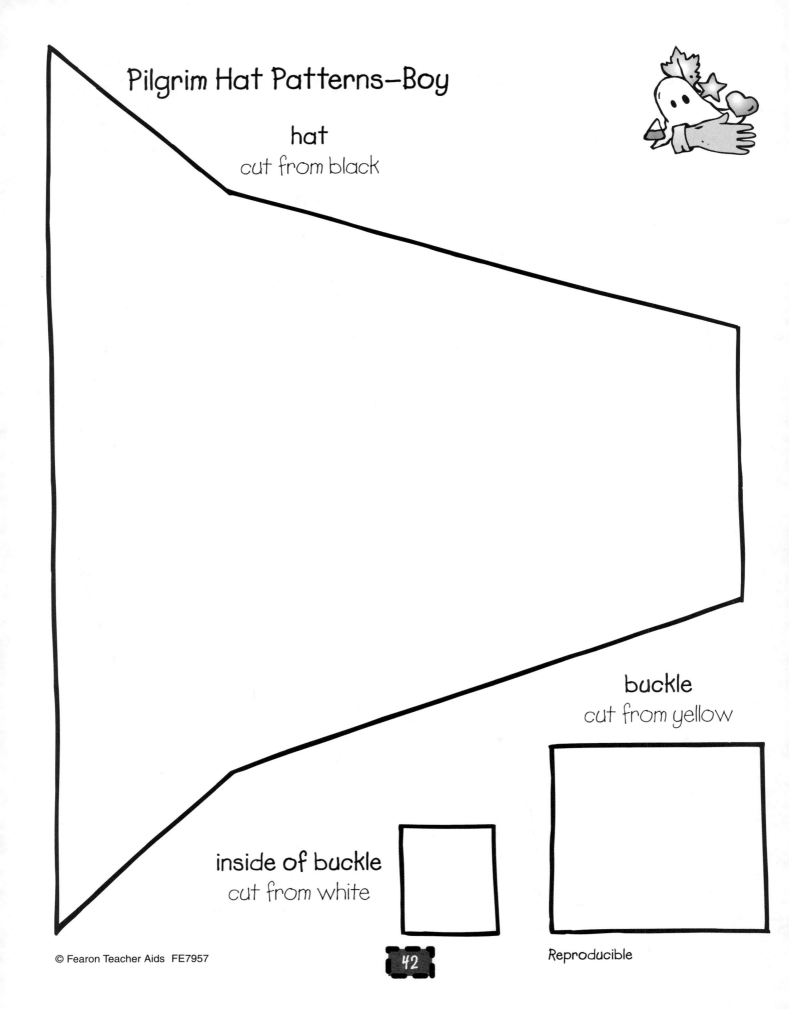

buckle
cut from yellow

inside of buckle
cut from white

42

Santa Hat Pattern

hat
cut 2 from red

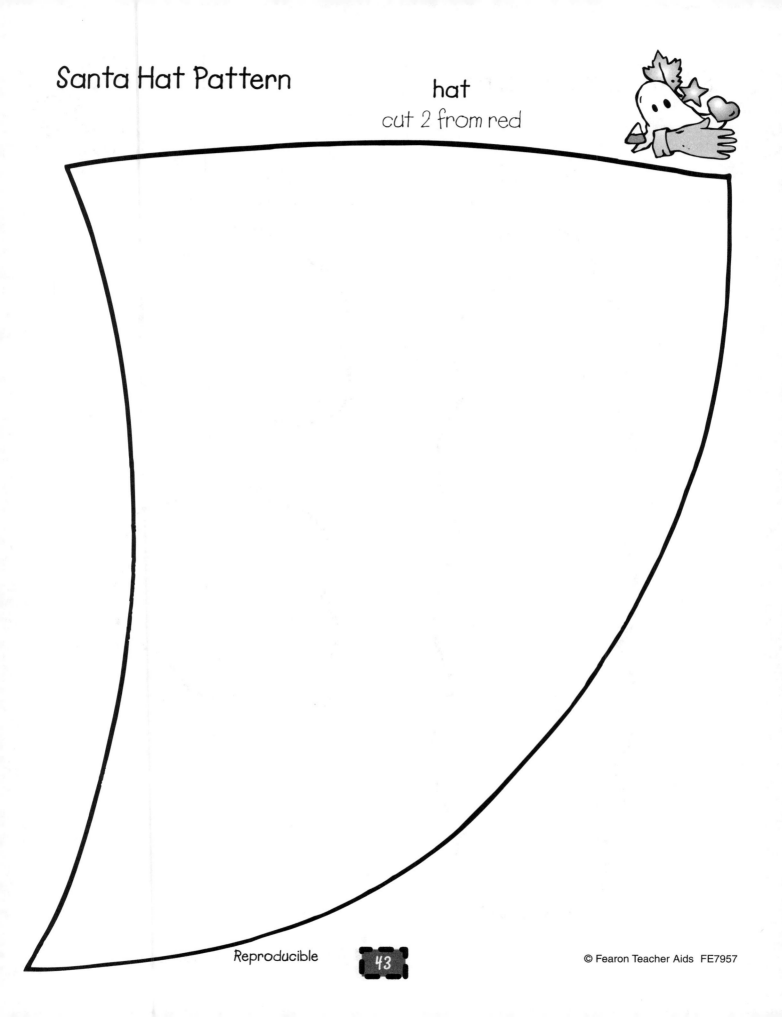

Santa Hat Patterns

hat band
cut 2 from white

pom pom
cut from white

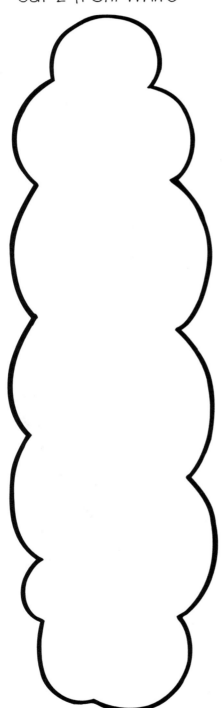

Hand Patterns

hands
cut from skin-tone colors,
pink, beige, light and dark brown

Heart Patterns

hearts
cut from white, pink and red

46

Flag and Firework Patterns

flag
cut from white

fireworks
cut from white

Nighttime

Scenery:

Paint a nighttime mural on bulletin-board paper. Using white paper, have students sponge paint the background with shades of dark blue. The moon and stars can be painted directly onto the mural or children can cut shapes from patterns, sprinkle with glitter and then glue them onto the mural. Stars can be arranged to represent common constellations such as the Big Dipper. Nighttime mobiles can also be made and hung from the ceiling. (See instructions on page 52.)

Costumes:

1. Nighttime hats. (See instructions on page 52.)

2. Children can dress in pajamas and carry or place stuffed animals on stage.

Presentation:

Divide the class into six groups. Assign one song to each group. All groups sing opening and closing songs. Individual groups sing assigned songs. If desired, the students singing "Star" or "Nightlight" songs can use flashlights to blink on and off at the appropriate times.

Related Books To Share With Your Class:

A Space Story by Karla Kuskin. (Harper, 1978).

Beyond the Milky Way by Cecile Schoberle. (Crown, 1986).

Dikou and the Baby Star by Elzbieta. (Harper, 1988).

Goodnight Moon by Margaret Wise Brown. (Harper, 1947).

Maggie's Moon by Martha Alexander. (Dial, 1982).

Moon Man by Tomi Ungerer. (Harper, 1967).

Our Solar System by Cindy Barden. (Teacher Created Materials, 1997).

Papa, Please Get the Moon for Me by Eric Carle. (Picture Book, 1985).

The Lunatic Adventure of Kitman and Willy by Chris Demarest. (Simon & Schuster, 1988).

The Moon by Robert Louis Stevenson. (Harper, 1984).

The Night Book by Mark Strand. (Crown, 1985).

Opening Song:

Nighttime
(Sung to the tune "Kookaburra")

Nighttime is my favorite time of day,
When the sunlight starts to slip away.
The stars are a'twinkling,
And the moon is a'blinking.
It's my favorite time of day.

Nighttime is my favorite time of day.
Time to put my skates and bike away.
The popcorn is popping,
By the TV I'll be stopping.
It's my favorite time of day.

Nighttime is my favorite time of day.
Guess I'll go to sleep, there's no more time to play.
The stars are a'twinkling,
And the moon is a'blinking.
It's my favorite time of day.

Group 1:

The Moon
(Sung to the tune "Twinkle, Twinkle")

When I look up at the sky,
Something special I do spy.
The moon is shining big and bright.
Orange and round it's quite a sight!
But when I look another night,
Someone took a great big bite!

The Stars

(Sung to the tune "How Much Is That Doggie In The Window?")

Group 2:

The stars up in the sky are shining brightly.
They twinkle and light up the sky.
I'll make a special wish upon that big one.
I hope it comes true by and by.

The Sleepover

(Sung to the tune "Bringing Home a Baby Bumble Bee")

Group 3:

Mom says I can sleep at Ted's tonight.
Oh, what fun! We'll have a pillow fight.
We'll stay up late, eat chips, and pizza, too.
Sneak behind his sister and then shout "boo!"

My Teddy

(Sung to the tune "Down By the Station")

Group 4:

When it's time to go to bed,
I like to grab my Teddy.
His ear is torn. His nose is gone.
He's quite a sight to see.
You might have a dog or cat,
But I'll keep my old Teddy.
I'll hold him tight and close my eyes and soon
I'm fast asleep.

Reproducible

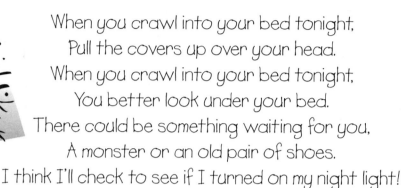

Group 5:

The Night Light

(Sung to the tune "Teddy Bear's Picnic")

When you crawl into your bed tonight,
Pull the covers up over your head.
When you crawl into your bed tonight,
You better look under your bed.
There could be something waiting for you,
A monster or an old pair of shoes.
I think I'll check to see if I turned on my night light!

Group 6:

Dreams

(Sung to the tune "Oh Where, Oh Where Has My Little Dog Gone?")

I like to dream when I go to sleep
Of flying high over the trees.
I can swim with a whale
Holding on to his tail
And stay up all night if I please!

Closing Song:

Repeat Opening Song

Directions for hats and mobile:

Hats: Cut two-2" x 12" (5cm x 30cm) pieces of dark blue construction paper. Use the patterns on page 53. Have students cut out stars and moon pattern. Glue them in a pattern along the length of the band. Decorate the stars and moons. The stars can be painted with a diluted glue mixture. Then sprinkle with glitter. Fit bands to the students' heads.

Mobile:

Follow directions above to decorate a 2" x 18" (5cm x 45cm) band of dark blue construction paper. Glue or staple together to form a ring. Punch three evenly spaced holes around the top edge to attach strings for hanging the mobile. Punch four evenly spaced holes around the bottom edge to attach celestial objects such as the moon, stars, planets, and clouds. Attach the objects using different lengths of string. Attach three strings of identical length to the top holes. Tie together at the top. Attach a paper clip or other hanger.

Hat Patterns

full moon
cut from white

crescent moon
cut from white

star
cut from white

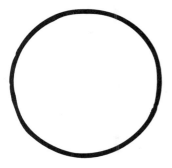

Mobile Pattern

moon
cut from yellow

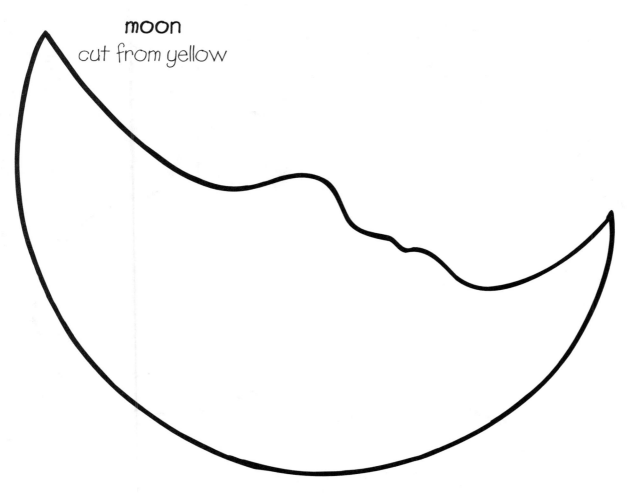

Mobile Patterns

star

cut from yellow

cloud

cut from white

54

Mobile Patterns

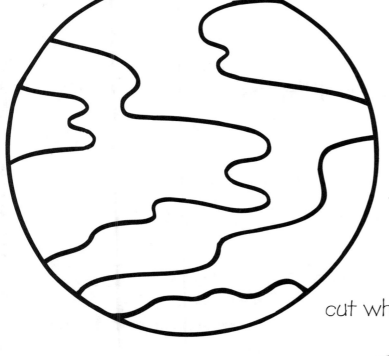

planets
cut white paper and color as desired

Whatever the Weather

Scenery:

Have the students paint, draw or use color to create each individual weather condition on separate pieces of bulletin-board paper. Hang these papers on the wall to use as backdrops.

Costumes:

1. Have students dress in various shades of blue to represent the sky.

2. Make weather hats. (See instructions on pages 61 to 62.)

Presentation:

Divide the class into the six weather conditions. Have groups sing the opening song together in one large group. As each song is presented, the group depicting that weather condition comes forward, stands in front of their mural and sings their song. Groups come together at the end to sing the closing song.

Related Books To Share With Your Class:

All Wet! All Wet! by James Skofield. (Harper, 1984).

Cloudy with a Chance of Meatballs by Judi Barrett. (Atheneum, 1978).

Dr. Bartholomew and the Oobleck by Dr. Seuss. (Random, 1949).

It's Snowing! It's Snowing! by Jack Prelutsky.
  (Greenwillow, 1984).

Peter Spier's Rain by Peter Spier. (Doubleday, 1982).

Rainy Sunday by Eleanor Schick. (Dial, 1982).

Snowy Day by Ezra J. Keats. (Viking, 1962).

Snow is Falling by Franklyn M. Branley. (Harper, 1986).

The Snowman by Raymond Briggs. (Random House, 1978).

Sun, Rain by Niki Yektai. (Macmillan, 1984).

Weather

(Sung to the tune "Teddy Bear Picnic")

If you go out on a sunny day,
The weather will make you grin.
If you go out on a stormy day,
You might have to rush back in.
The sun, the clouds, the rain and the snow,
The weather can change,
Wherever you go.
Be sure you check, before you dress,
For the weather.

Group 1:

Sun

(Sung to the tune "Kookabura")

The sun shines down from the bright blue sky,
Bringing us light as the day goes by.
We love the sun,
It shines on everyone,
A sunny day's so fine.

Group 2:

Clouds
(Sung to the tune "Up on the Housetop")

When I look up into the sky,
Many clouds go rolling by,
I spy a rabbit, a fox, a tree.
Clouds can look different to you and me.
Clouds in the sky, rolling by.
Clouds so high, what do you spy?
Oh, when I look up into the sky,
Many clouds go rolling by.

Group 3:

A Windy Day
(Sung to the tune "Farmer in the Dell")

I love a windy day.
It blows my hat away.
I can fly my kite,
'Til it's out of sight,
On a windy, windy day.

Reproducible

Storms

(Sung to the tune "I'm a Little Teapot")

When the wind blows,
And I look outside,
Thunder booms, lightning breaks the sky.
The clouds turn black,
And the rain begins to fall.
A storm is coming.
Fall, rain, fall.

Group 5:

Snow

(Sung to the tune "Row, Row, Row")

Snow, snow, snow tonight,
I really hope it will.
Building snowmen, sledding too,
I'll soar right down the hill.

Snow, snow, snow tonight,
I'll see it when I wake.
Making angels, skating too,
I'll glide around the lake.

Group 6:

Rainbow

(Sung to the tune "My Bonnie Lies over the Ocean")

As the storm is ending,
A beautiful arch in the sky,
A rainbow is on the horizon,
A colorful sight to my eye.
Rainbow, rainbow,
A ribbon of color for you and me,
Rainbow, rainbow,
A wonderful sight to see.

 Closing Song:

Repeat Opening Song

Directions for hats:

Cut two 2" x 12" (5cm x 30cm) pieces of construction paper and fit to the students' heads.

Sun: Copy patterns from pages 63 to 64 onto construction paper. Glue sun onto sunray. Glue face features onto sun. Staple or glue completed sun to headband.

Clouds: Copy patterns from page 65 onto construction paper. Sponge paint the clouds using very light shades of pink and blue. After clouds are dry, cut them out and staple or glue to headband.

Wind: Copy pattern from page 66 onto construction paper. Use chalk to create the illusion of blowing wind. Staple or glue to headband.

Storms: Copy patterns from pages 67 to 68 onto construction paper. Use black marker to trace over the word *boom*. Glue or staple lightning, gray cloud and the word *boom* to the headband. Punch holes in rain drops. Tie string to raindrops, then punch holes in the headband. Attach raindrops to the headband.

Snow: Copy patterns from page 69 onto construction paper. Show students how to fold circles into quarters. Show them how to snip folded edges to make snowflakes. Dab with glue and sprinkle with silver glitter. Cut out and glue or staple to headband.

Rainbow: Copy pattern from page 70 onto construction paper. Use markers, crayons or paint to color the rainbow—red, orange, yellow, green, blue, and purple. Staple or glue to headband.

Sun Hat Pattern

sunray
cut from orange

Sun Hat Patterns

sun
cut from yellow

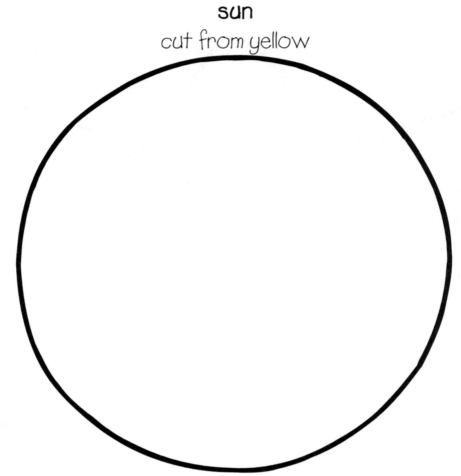

face on sun
cut from black

Reproducible

Cloud Hat Patterns

clouds
cut from white

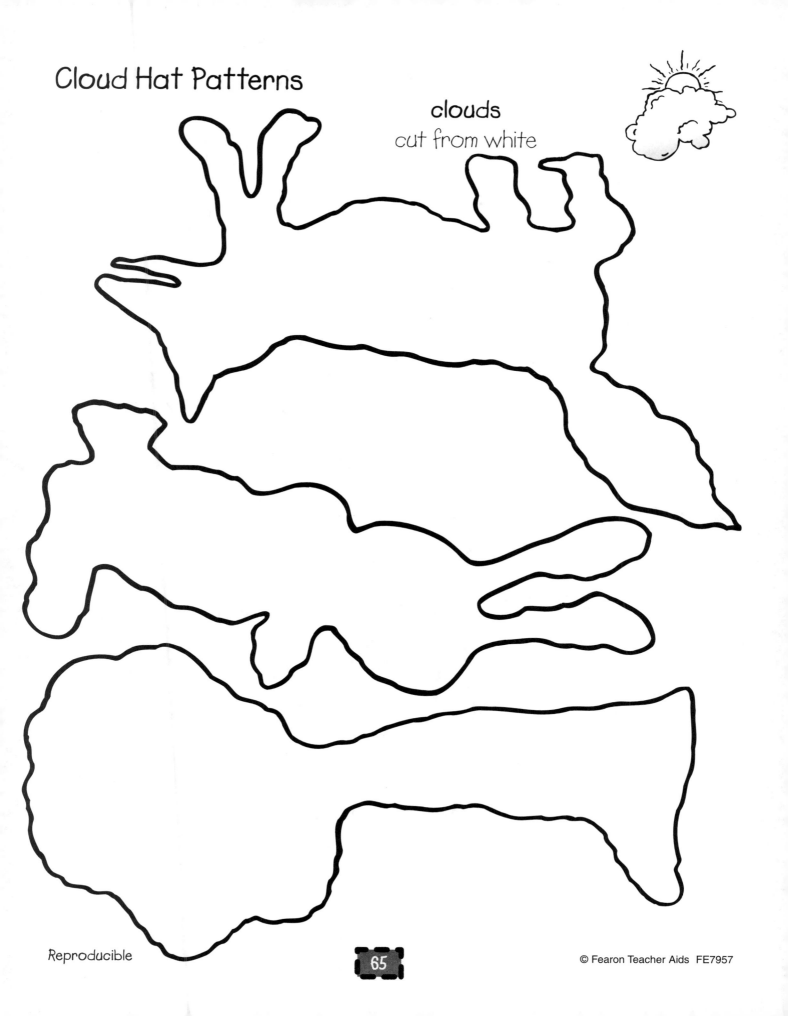

Wind Hat Pattern

wind
cut from white or light blue

Reproducible

Storm Hat Patterns

lightning bolt
cut from yellow

cloud
cut from gray

© Fearon Teacher Aids FE7957

Storm Hat Patterns

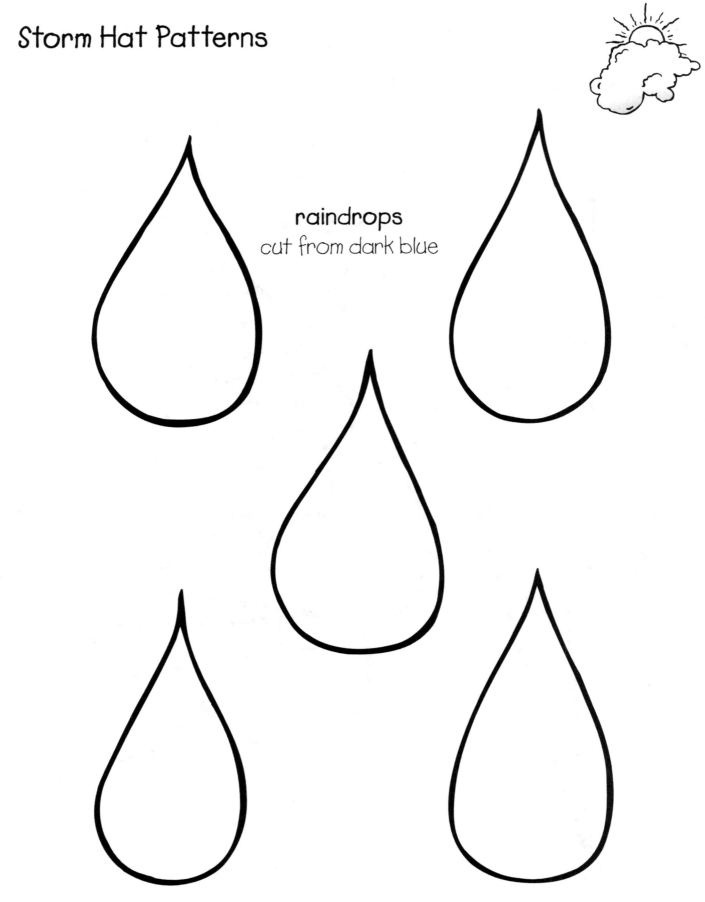

raindrops
cut from dark blue

68

Reproducible

Snow Hat Patterns

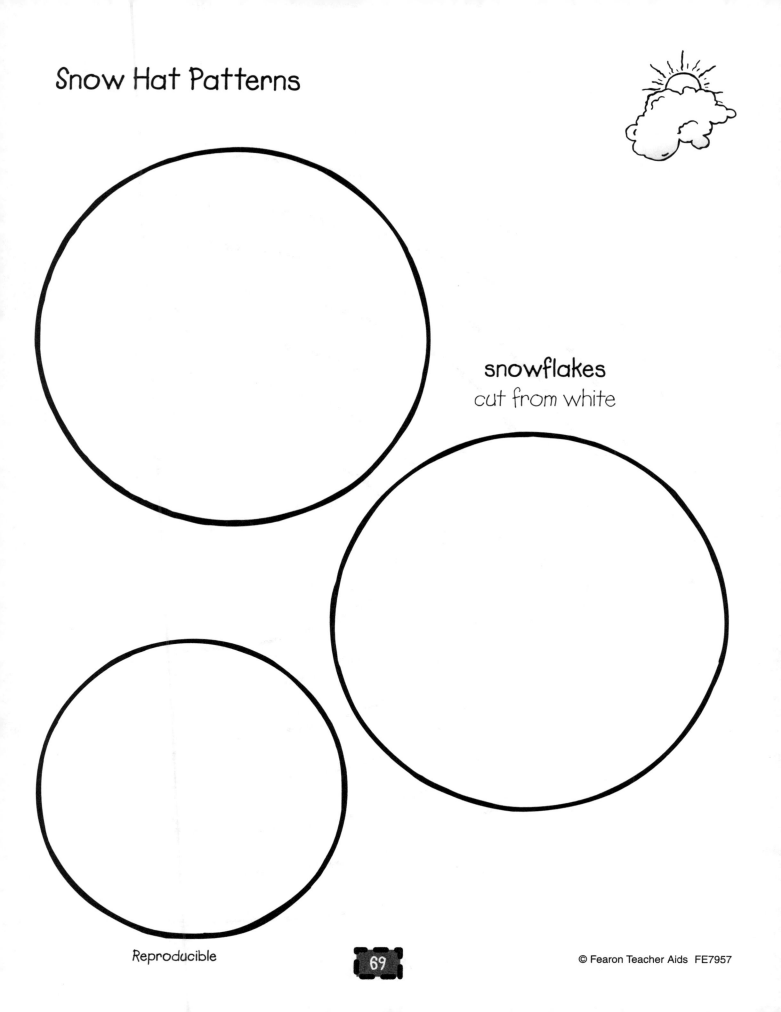

snowflakes
cut from white

Rainbow Hat Pattern

rainbow

cut from white

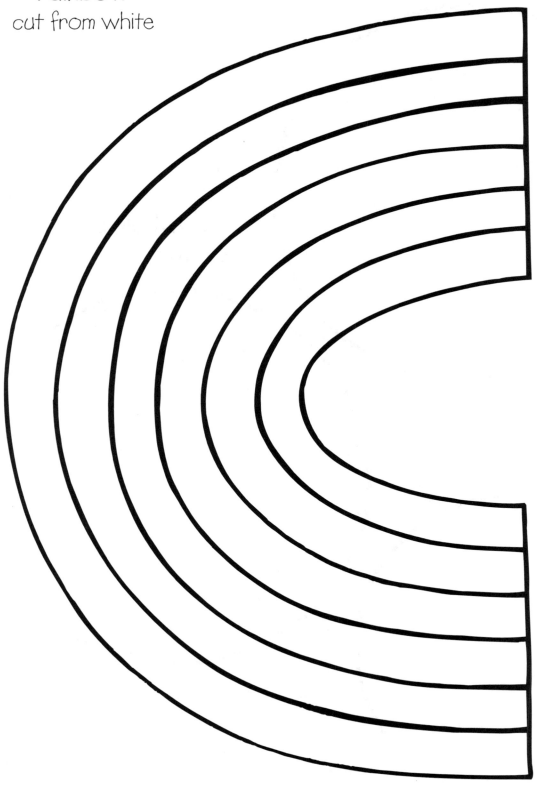

Reproducible

The Ladybug Ball

Scenery:

Have students imagine they are tiny insects in someone's yard. They can paint a mural of what it might look like from an insect's point of view. They could include tall grasses, weeds, flowers, mushrooms, and even a giant lawn mower or rake at the edge of the mural.

Costumes:

Make insect character bibs and hats. (See instructions on pages 75 to 78.)

Presentation:

The Ladybug Ball could be acted out as a play. Individual students can play the six main characters. Several students can play the role of the ants and act out their parts as the class sings. If you choose to present the program as a play, you will need additional props, such as a table for refreshments, play food, a cardboard or real fiddle for the cricket, a chair for the ladybug to sit on, and a net to be used as the spider's web.

The class can be divided into six groups with all students in a group wearing the appropriate character bibs for that insect. All students sing opening and closing songs while individual groups sing the songs for their designated insects.

Related Books To Share With Your Class:

Albert & Veronica by Deborah Gangloff. (Crown, 1989).

A House of Leaves by Kiyoshi Soya. (Putnam, 1987).

Bugs! by Patricia and Fredrick McKissack. (Childrens, 1988).

Chester Cricket's Pigeon Ride and *Chester Cricket's New Home* by George Selden. (Bantam Doubleday, 1981, 1984).

Company's Coming by Arthur Yorinks. (Crown, 1988).

Little Bug by Dick Gackenbach. (Houghton, 1981).

Lucky Me by Denys Cazet. (Bradbury, 1983).

Maggie and the Pirate by Ezra Jack Keats. (Macmillan, 1987).

The Grouchy Ladybug by Eric Carle. (Harper, 1977).

The Very Busy Spider by Eric Carle. (Putnam, 1981).

When It Comes to Bugs: Poems by Aileen Fisher. (Harper, 1986).

The Ladybug Ball

(Sung to the tune "My Bonnie Lies Over the Ocean")

Opening Song:

The Ladybug Ball is this evening.
We welcome you all to the dance.
The guests are now arriving.
There's Butterfly, Spider, and Ant.

Beetle, Cricket,
They're all coming out for the Ladybug Ball.
Grasshopper, Bumble Bee,
It's time now. Come one and come all.

Group 1:

Ladybug

(Sung to the tune "She'll be Comin' Around the Mountain")

She'll be rocking and a' rolling at the dance.
She'll be running and a' chasing those bad ants.
That old ladybug's so busy,
Running 'round in such a tizzy.
It's not easy to be hostess at the dance.

Group 2:

Cricket
(Sung to the tune "Turkey in the Straw")

Oh, the cricket plays the music at the Ladybug Ball.
It's time to dance. Come one, come all.
He fiddles with his legs and the music's mighty fine.
Come on down for a really good time!

Cricket plays music for the dance.
Everyone joins in, even those ants.
You all come down and join the fun.
The Ladybug Ball's for everyone!

Group 3:

Butterfly
(Sung to the tune "Edelweiss")

Butterfly, butterfly,
Floating across the dance floor.
Graceful and free,
Lovely is she—
Queen of the Ladybug Ball.

Watch as her shimmering wings pass by,
Sparkling in the sunset.
Graceful and free,
Lovely is she—
Queen of the Ladybug Ball.

Group 4:

Ants

(Sung to the tune "The Ants Come Marching")

The ants come marching into the ball, hurray, hurray.
The ants come marching into the ball. Put the food away.
They'll eat all the cake and drink the punch, too.
What is poor Ladybug to do?
When the ants come marching into the Ladybug Ball.

Group 5:

Spider

(Sung to the tune "The Eensy Weensy Spider")

The big, black, ugly spider sneaks into the ball.
When no one is looking, up the wall he crawls.
He waits until the ladybug sits down beneath his web,
Then the big, black, ugly spider jumps down upon her head.

Group 6:

Bumble Bee

(Sung to the tune "Yankee Doodle")

Someone's caught in the spider's web.
Who will save the day?
Handsome in his striped suit,
Bee is on his way.
Bumble Bee is here to stay.
Bumble Bee's a winner.
He came in to save the day.
Got spider with his stinger.

Reproducible

Ladybug Ball
(Sung to the tune "My Bonnie Lies Over the Ocean")

We hope you had fun at the ball.
It's time to go home now you see.
The insects have left the party
And all that is left here is me.
Goodbye, goodbye,
We hope that you really enjoyed the show.
Goodbye, goodbye,
It's time now for you to go!

Directions for Character Bibs and Hats

Make character bibs from the patterns by following the directions. When completed, punch a hole on each side of the bib, near the top. Attach strings, yarn or ribbons so students can wear the character bibs around their necks.

Ladybug: To make the ladybug's body fold a 12" x 18" (30cm x 45cm) sheet of black construction paper into quarters. Cut along a curved line as shown. Unfold the paper.

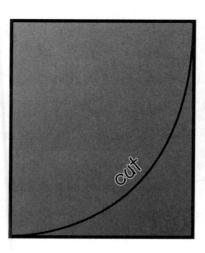

75

For the ladybug's wings, repeat the previous directions using red paper. Open the paper so it is folded in half lengthwise. Cut along curved line on the folded edge as shown. Unfold and glue to ladybug body. Arrange six black dots on the wings and glue. Punch holes on both sides of the body and attach strings so students can wear around their necks.

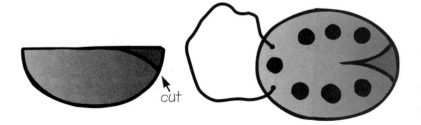

cut

Cricket: Cut the following pattern from a 12" x 18" (30cm x 45cm) piece of brown or black construction paper folded in half lengthwise.

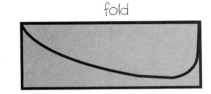

fold

Use the patterns on page 79 to make three sets of legs. Glue three legs to each side as shown. The largest pair should be attached to the bottom portion of the cricket. Punch holes on both sides of the body and attach strings so students can wear around their necks.

Butterfly: Trace the butterfly wings pattern (page 80) onto a 12" x 18" (30cm x 45cm) piece of construction paper folded in half. Let students choose from a variety of bright colors. Cut out and decorate as desired. Cut out the butterfly body (page 81) from black construction paper and glue to the wings. Punch a hole on both sides of the wings and attach strings so students can wear around their necks.

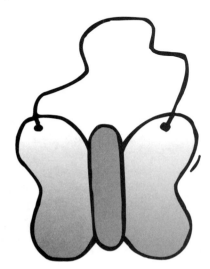

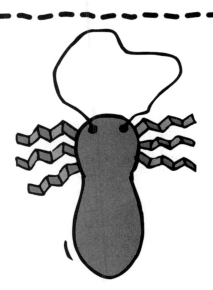

Ant: Cut the following shape from a piece of 12" x 18" (30cm x 45cm) brown construction paper. Use six 1" x 5" (2cm x 12cm) strips of black construction paper. Accordian-fold and attach three on each side of the top section for legs. Punch holes on both sides of the body near the top. Attach strings so students can wear around their necks.

Spider: Using black construction paper, follow step one for ladybug body (page 75). Use eight 1" x 12" (2cm x 30cm) pieces of black construction paper. Accordian-fold and attach four to each side of body. Punch holes on both sides of the body. Attach strings so students can wear around their necks.

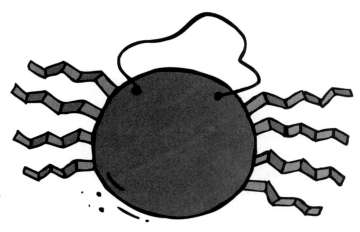

Bumble bee: From a 12" x 18" (30cm x 45cm) piece of yellow construction paper cut a shape identical to that of the ant. Use 1¼" (3cm) strips of black construction paper for stripes. Glue stripes to the body. Make a triangular-shaped stinger from black paper and glue to the bottom of the body. Cut out and glue large circles on each side of the bee for wings. Punch holes on both sides of the head and attach strings so students can wear around their necks.

Insect Hats: Cut two 2" x 12" (5cm x 30cm) pieces of black construction paper and fit to the students' heads. Accordian-fold two 1" x 5" (2cm x 12cm) pieces of black construction paper to represent antennae. Glue to the front of the headband. All characters except the spider wear this hat.

Spider Hat: Make headbands. Cut a black circle from the pattern on page 81. Glue to headband to represent the spider's head.

Cricket Leg Patterns

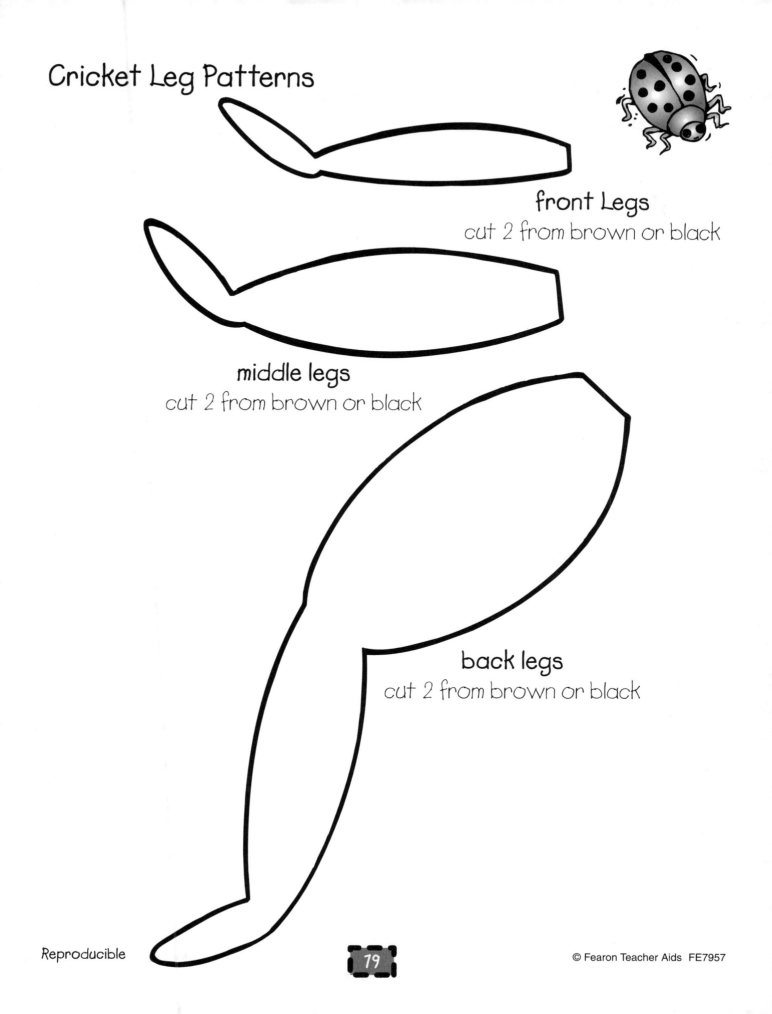

front Legs
cut 2 from brown or black

middle legs
cut 2 from brown or black

back legs
cut 2 from brown or black

Butterfly Wing Pattern

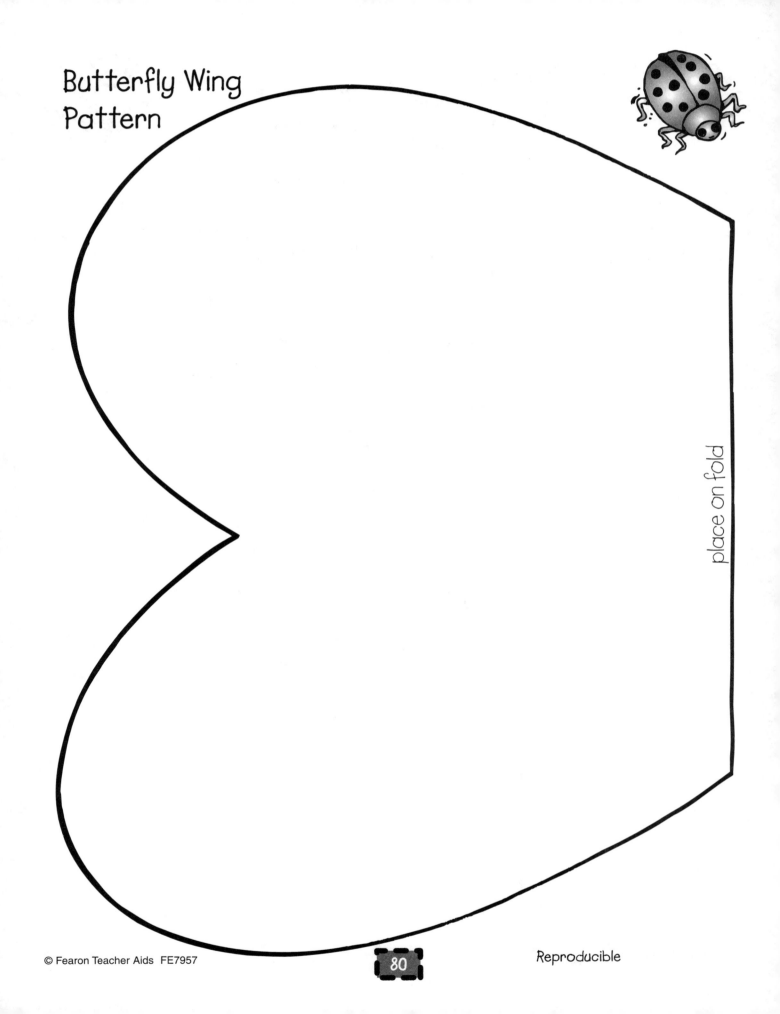

place on fold

80

Reproducible

Butterfly and Spider Patterns

butterfly body
cut from black

spider
cut from black

Our Five Senses

Scenery:

Divide students into five groups. Assign one of the five senses (smell, touch, hearing, taste, sight) to each group. On separate sheets of paper, have students paint or draw objects representing the sense assigned to their group. Cut out the objects and glue them to a large piece of bulletin-board paper. Hang on the wall and use as a backdrop.

Costumes:

Make senses hats. (See instructions on page 86.)

Presentation:

The class as a whole can sing the songs while groups of students are designated as the five different senses. As the class sings about the sense, those children representing that sense come forward and perform actions to the song.

Related Books To Share With Your Class:

Bunny Sees, Duckling Sees, Puppy Sees, Little Lamb Sees (four books) by Hargrave Hands. (Putnam, 1985).

Find Out By Touching by Paul Showers. (Harper, 1961).

I Hear, I See, and *I Touch* (three books) by Rachel Isadora. (Greenwillow, 1985).

I Hear, I See, and *I Touch* (three books) by Helen Oxenbury. (Random, 1986).

My Five Senses by Aliki. (Harper, 1962).

The Five Senses-Hearing, Sight, Smell, Taste, and *Touch* (five books) by J.M. Parramon. (Barron's, 1985).

Touch Will Tell by Marcia Brown. (Watts, 1979).

Your Five Senses by Ray Broekel. (Childrens, 1964).

Your Nose and Ears by Joan Iveson-Iveson. (Watts, 1985).

Our Five Senses

(Sung to the tune "She'll Be Comin' Around the Mountain")

We can see and hear and smell and taste and touch.
We can see and hear and smell and taste and touch.
Our five senses are amazing,
Something everyone is praising,
We can see and hear and smell and taste and touch.

Group 1:

Smell

(Sung to the tune "Yankee Doodle")

I'm so glad to have my nose,
There's such great things to smell:
Chocolate chip cookies and a red, red, rose,
There's more that I can tell.
Pizza, pie and pancakes too,
All the scents of spring,
I'm so glad to have my nose,
I'll smell most anything.

Group 2:

Taste

(Sung to the tune "Farmer in the Dell")

Candy bars, ice cream, and cake,
Are things I like to taste.
They tickle my tongue,
Make my tummy shout YUM!
Candy bars, ice cream, and cake,

Apples and peaches and peas,
Are all so good for me.
They're healthy too,
So good for you!
Apples and peaches and peas.

Group 3:

Touch

(Sung to the tune "Jack and Jill")

Rough and smooth,
And bumpy and soft,
My fingers like to feel.
I'm so glad,
My sense of touch,
Makes everything so real.

Group 4:

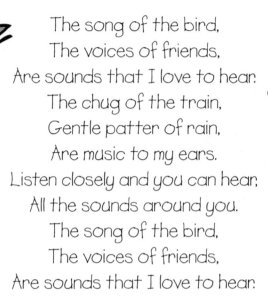

Hearing
(Sung to the tune "Edelweiss")

The song of the bird,
The voices of friends,
Are sounds that I love to hear.
The chug of the train,
Gentle patter of rain,
Are music to my ears.
Listen closely and you can hear,
All the sounds around you.
The song of the bird,
The voices of friends,
Are sounds that I love to hear.

Sight
(Sung to the tune "This Old Man")

Group 5:

I see you. You see me.
There's so much our eyes can see.
We see fish and cats,
And birdies with their wings.
With our eyes we see great things.

I see color. I see light.
We see things both dull and bright.
We see trees and flowers,
And water in the stream.
With our eyes we all can dream.

Closing Song: Repeat Opening Song.

Directions for Senses Hats:

Cut two 2" x 12" (5cm x 30cm) pieces of construction paper and fit to the students' heads.

Smell: Copy nose pattern from page 87 onto construction paper. Use any color paper for nose. Glue or staple to headband.

Taste: Copy mouth patterns from page 88 onto construction paper. Glue tongue onto mouth. Glue or staple to headband.

Hearing: Copy ear patterns from page 89 onto construction paper. Glue or staple to headband.

Sight: Copy eye patterns from page 90 onto construction paper. Have students color eyes the same color as their own. Glue eyes to white background. Glue black pupils to eyes. Staple or glue to hat.

Touch: Have students trace their hands on construction paper. Cut out and curl fingers. Staple or glue to hat.

Smell Hat Pattern

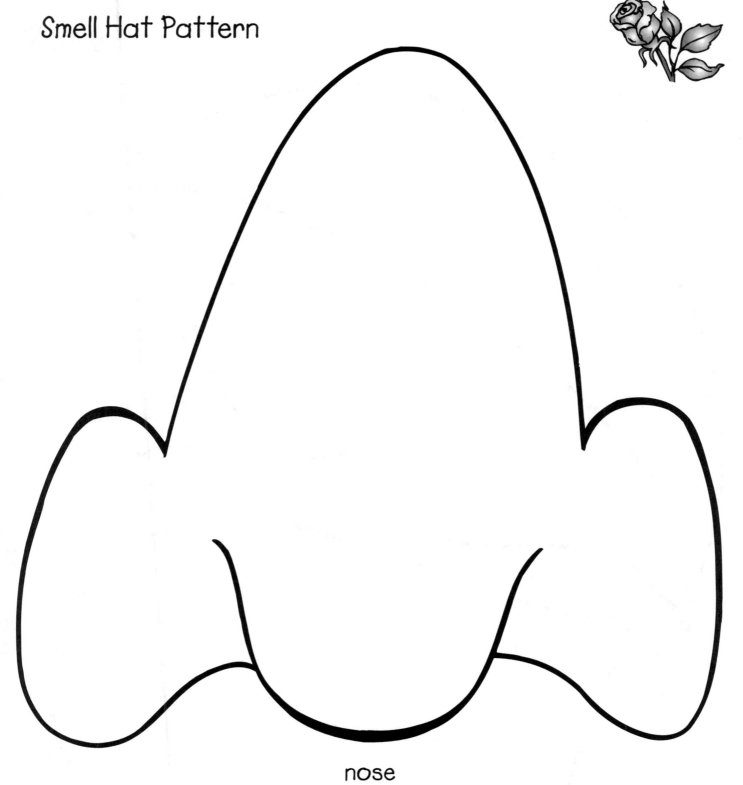

nose
cut from pink, beige or brown

© Fearon Teacher Aids FE7957

Taste Hat Patterns

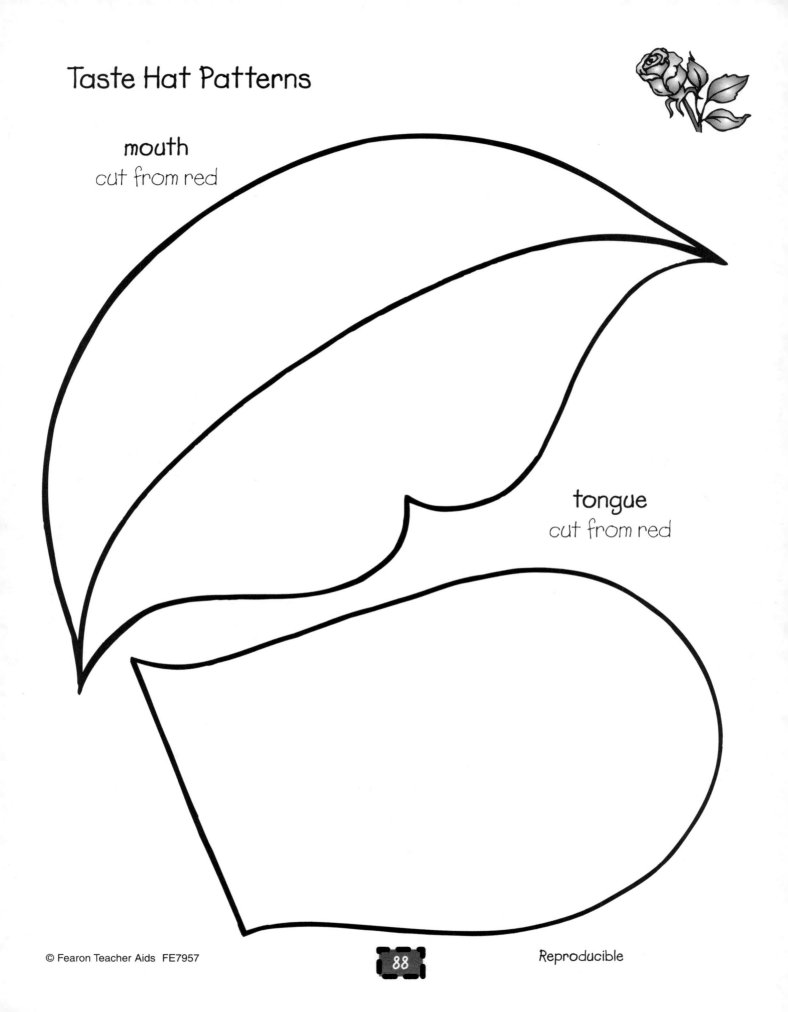

mouth
cut from red

tongue
cut from red

© Fearon Teacher Aids FE7957

Reproducible

Hearing Hat Patterns

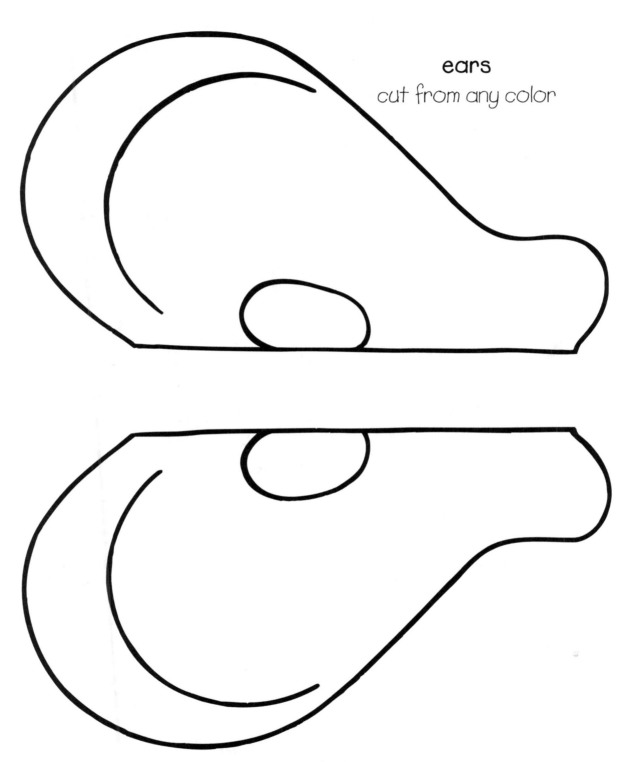

ears
cut from any color

Sight Hat Patterns

eye
cut 2 from white

pupil
cut 2 from black

eye background
cut 2 from white

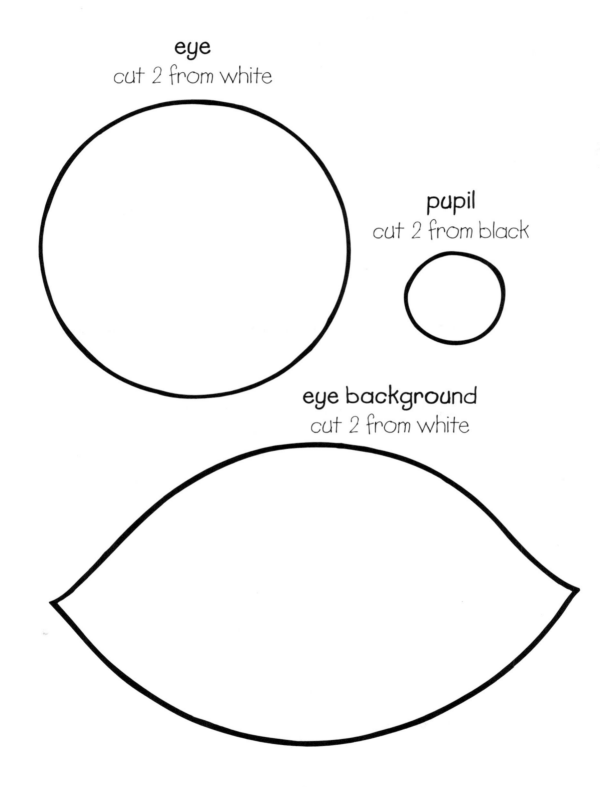

Reproducible

A Trip to the Zoo

Scenery:

Paint a zoo mural on bulletin-board paper. Hang it on the wall and use it as a backdrop. Cover or paint boxes of various sizes. Use strips of black paper for "bars" and put stuffed zoo animals inside. Arrange the "cages" around the room or stage.

Costumes:

Make animal character bibs and zookeeper hats. (See instructions on pages 95 to 96.)

Presentation:

The class as a whole can sing all of the songs. Assign students as the individual animals. As the class sings about an animal, those children representing that animal, come forward and perform animal actions to the side or in front of the group. Students in the group not assigned an animal part can wear zookeeper hats.

Alternate: The class can also be divided into six groups. Assign an animal to each group. All individuals in the group wear the animal bib for that animal. Groups sit in separate locations across the stage. Everyone sings the opening and ending songs. The individual groups sing the song for their designated animals.

Related Books To Share With Your Class:

1, 2, 3 To the Zoo: A Counting Book by Eric Carle. (Putnam, 1987).

A Children's Zoo by Tana Hoban. (Greenwillow, 1985).

Be Nice to Spiders by Margaret Graham. (Harper, 1967).

Cam Jansen and the Mystery at the Monkey House by David A. Adler. (Viking, 1985).

Curious George by H.A. Rey. (Houghton, 1941). See also other *Curious George* books by the same author.

Dear Zoo by Rod Campbell. (Macmillan, 1984).

Leo and Emily's Zoo by Franz Brandenberg. (Greenwillow, 1988).

The A to Z Zoo by Cindy Barden. (Judy/Instructo, 1995).

Sam Who Never Forgets by Eve Rice. (Greenwillow, 1977).

Zoo for Mister Muster by Arnold Lobel. (Harper, 1962).

Zoo Song by Barbara Bottner. (Scholastic, 1987).

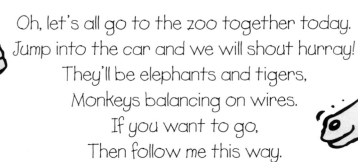

Zoo Song
(Sung to the tune "She'll Be Comin' Around the Mountain")

Oh, let's all go to the zoo together today.
Jump into the car and we will shout hurray!
They'll be elephants and tigers,
Monkeys balancing on wires.
If you want to go,
Then follow me this way.

Oh, let's all go to the zoo together today.
Ride the train and eat ice cream along the way.
There is always something new.
Do you want to come too?
Oh, let's all go to the zoo together today.

Group 1:

The Monkeys
(Sung to the tune "Playmate, Come Out and Play With Me")

Monkeys are so much fun to watch.
They see what I can do and then they do it too.
They swing from tree to tree,
Play hide and seek with me.
Let's find the monkey house and watch the show.

92

Reproducible

Group 2:

The Elephants
(Sung to the tune "Teddy Bear's Picnic")

The elephant is an amazing sight.
He swings his trunk as he walks.
His ears are too big and his tail's too small.
What would he say if he talked?
They're fun to watch as they march in a row,
Holding tails as they swing to and fro.
An elephant is quite an amazing creature!

Group 3:

The Lion
(Sung to the tune "The Yellow Star of Texas")

The lion in the zoo looks very fierce to me.
I would not climb into his cage or then his lunch I'd be.
I'll stay out here and watch him and when he opens wide,
I'll make a face and call him names then run away and hide!

Group 4:

The Kangaroo
(Sung to the tune "I'm a Little Teapot")

Mrs. Kangaroo how nice of you,
To give your child such a lovely view.
Everywhere you go she sits inside
Your cozy pocket and takes a ride.

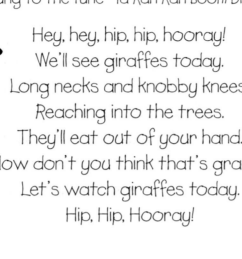

Group 5:

The Giraffe
(Sung to the tune "Ta Rah Rah Boom Di Ay")

Hey, hey, hip, hip, hooray!
We'll see giraffes today.
Long necks and knobby knees,
Reaching into the trees.
They'll eat out of your hand.
Now don't you think that's grand?
Let's watch giraffes today.
Hip, Hip, Hooray!

Song 6:

The Alligator
(Sung to the tune "Bringing Home a Baby Bumble Bee")

Alligator lying oh so still,
Alligator are you really real?
When the zoo keeper brings you your lunch
Down it goes with one big crunch!

Closing Song:

Zoo Song
(Sung to the tune "She'll Be Comin' Around the Mountain")

Well, we hope you had a good time at the zoo.
Where there's always lots of things for us to do.
Thanks for coming to our show.
Now it's time for us to go.
Well, we hope you had a good time at the zoo.

Reproducible

Directions for Animal Character Bibs:

Make character bibs from the patterns by following the directions. When completed, punch a hole on each side of the bib, near the top. Attach strings, yarn or ribbons so students can wear the character bibs around their necks.

Monkey: Copy patterns from pages 97 to 98 onto construction paper. Students may trace face pattern onto black paper. Glue face onto head. Glue nose and mouth piece and eyes onto face.

Optional: Coffee grounds can be glued on the outside portion of the head not covered by the face to resemble the appearance of hair.

Elephant: Copy patterns from pages 99 to 100 onto construction paper. Draw eyes on the head. Fold trunk on the dotted line and glue onto head. Glue ears to sides of the head. Glue legs to bottom of body. Cut a 1" x3" (2cm x 7cm) rectangle from scraps. Glue ends together to form a loop. Glue loop to back of head and attach head to body.

Lion: Copy patterns from pages 101 to 102 onto construction paper. Glue face onto mane. Glue eyes and nose onto face. Draw mouth.

Kangaroo: Copy patterns from page 103 onto construction paper. Glue eyes onto eye background. Glue to the face. Use a black marker to draw the nostrils on the face.

Giraffe: Copy patterns from pages 104 to 105 onto construction paper. Using a sponge and brown paint, sponge paint five or six spots on the giraffe's face. Glue horns to the top of the head. Fold eyelashes on the dotted line. Fringe the bottom half of the eyelashes and glue to the head placing glue on the unfringed portion of the eyelashes.

Alligator: Copy patterns from pages 106 to 107 onto construction paper. Glue eye to eye background. Glue to the head. Fold lower mouth section on the dotted line. Place glue on the folded section and glue the lower mouth to the alligator head so the bottom portion of both pieces match up. Fold teeth sections on the dotted lines. Glue one piece to each side of the lower mouth section.

Directions for Zookeeper Hat:

Cut two 2" x 12" (5cm x 30cm) pieces of construction paper and fit to the students' heads. Copy Zookeeper hat pattern (page 108) on white construction paper. Have students color or decorate as they choose. Cut out the pattern and glue to the front of the headband.

Monkey Pattern

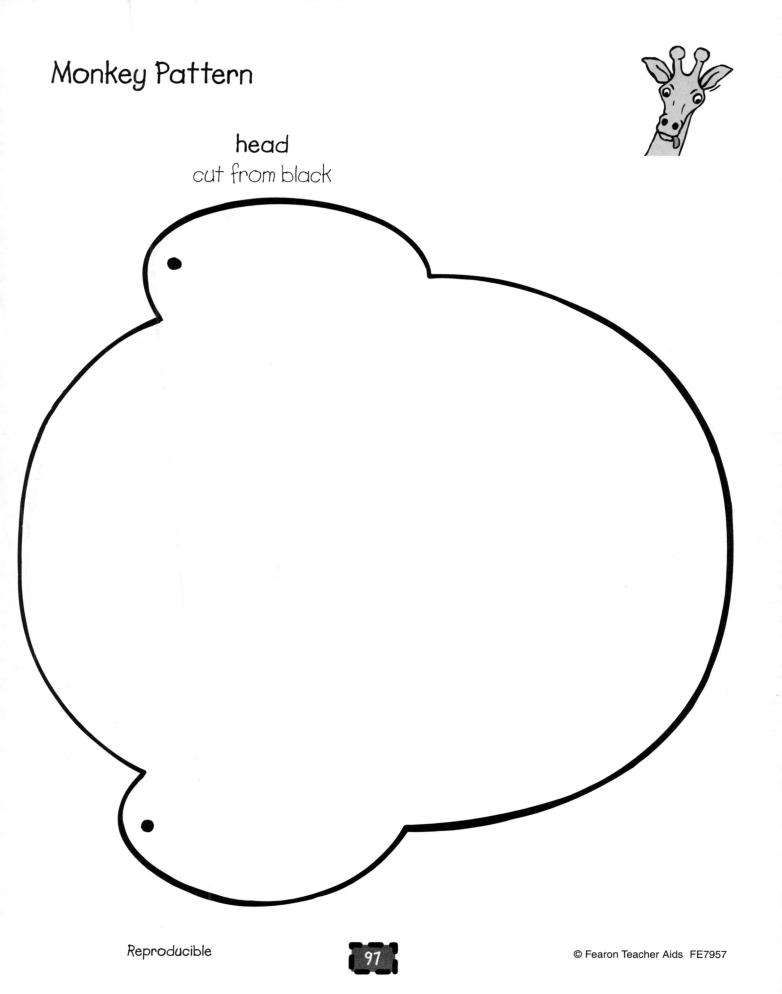

head
cut from black

Monkey Patterns

eyes
cut from black

background for eyes
cut from white

mouth and nose
cut from brown

face
cut from brown

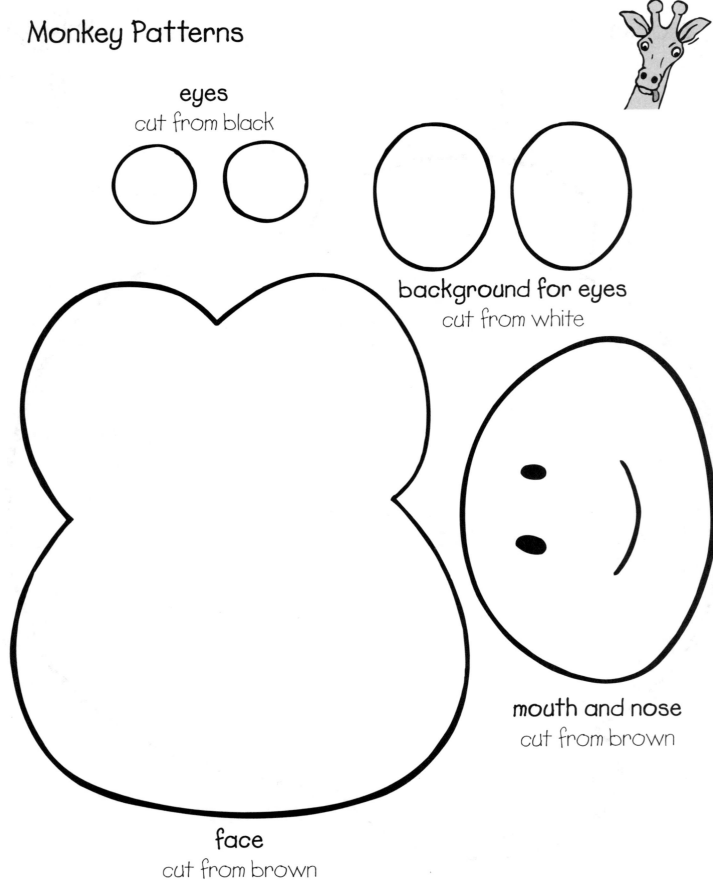

98

Elephant Patterns

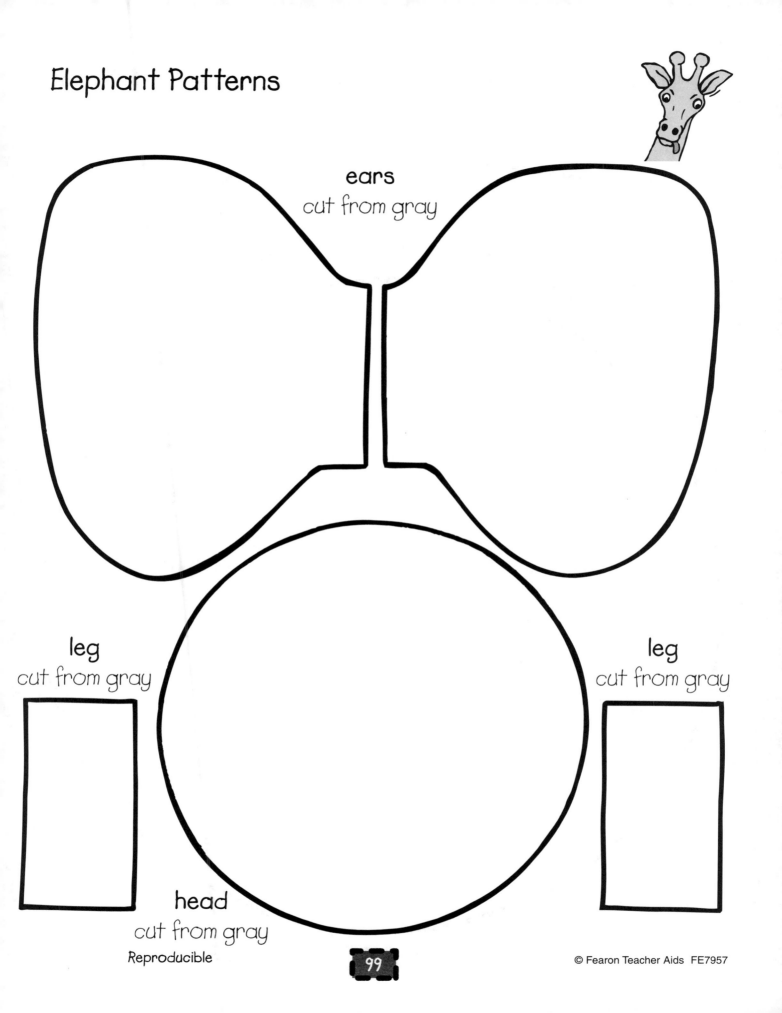

ears
cut from gray

leg
cut from gray

leg
cut from gray

head
cut from gray

Reproducible

Elephant Patterns

trunk
cut from gray

fold

body
cut from gray

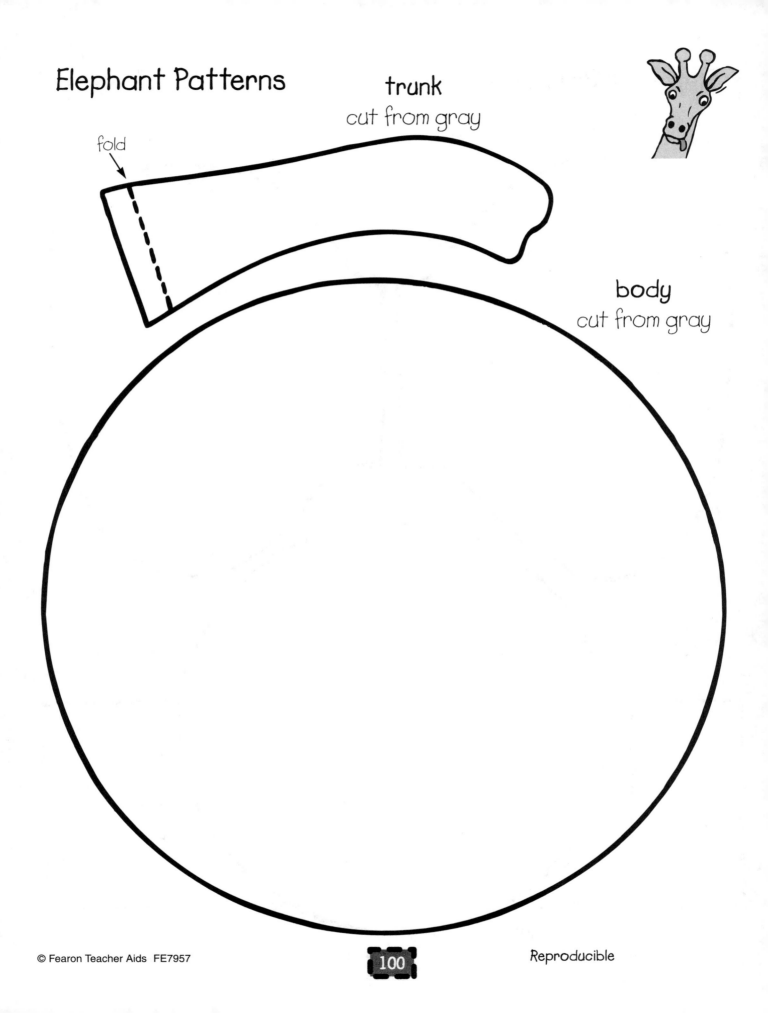

Reproducible

Lion Patterns

face
cut from yellow

eyes
cut from black

nose
cut from black

Lion Pattern

mane
cut from brown

102

Reproducible

Kangaroo Patterns

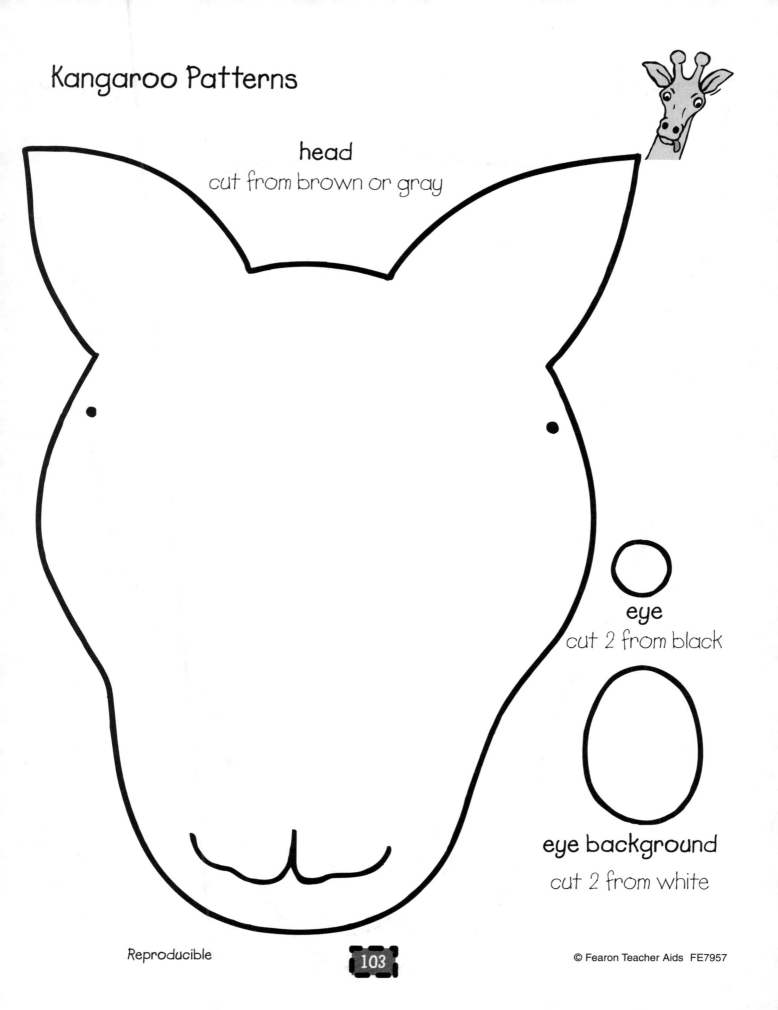

head
cut from brown or gray

eye
cut 2 from black

eye background
cut 2 from white

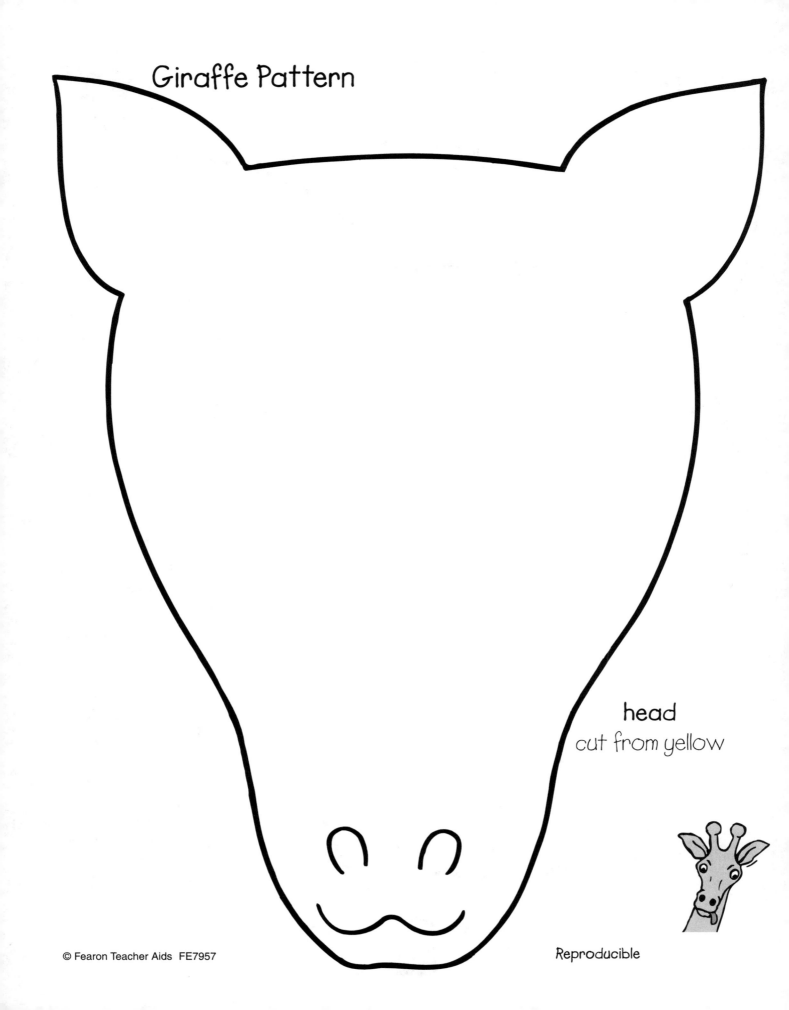

Giraffe Pattern

head
cut from yellow

Reproducible

Giraffe Patterns

horns
cut from black

eyelashes
cut from black

fold →   ← fold

Alligator Pattern

head
cut from green

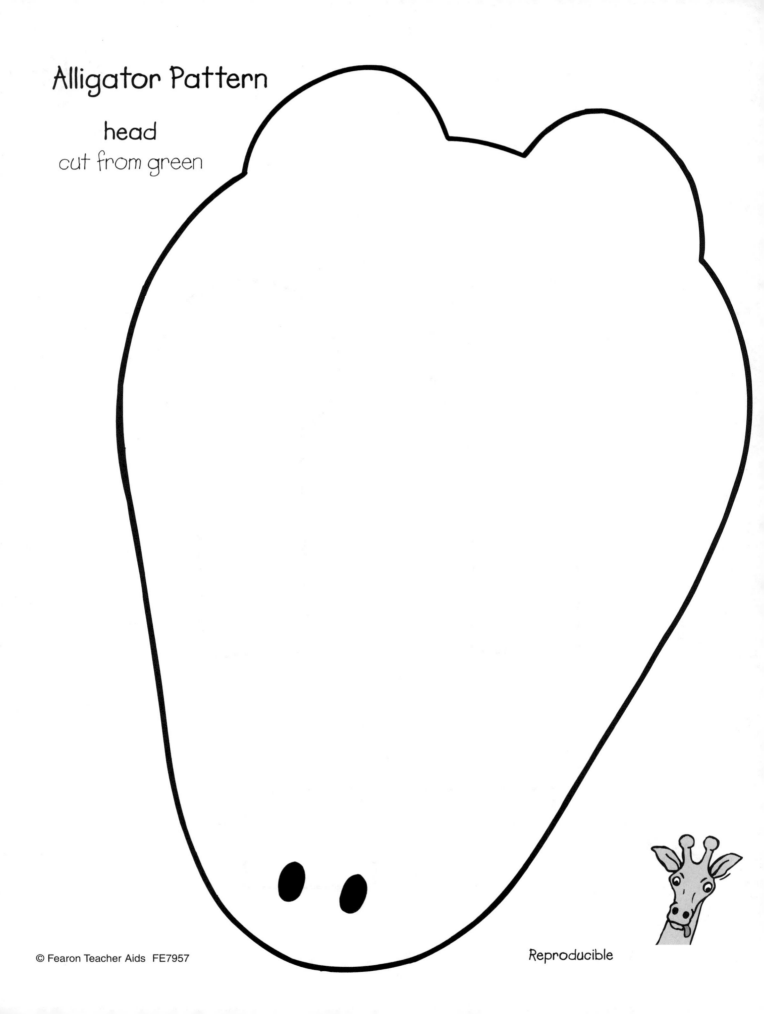

Reproducible

Alligator Patterns

mouth
cut from green

fold

eyes
cut from black

fold

fold

teeth
cut from white

eye background
cut from white

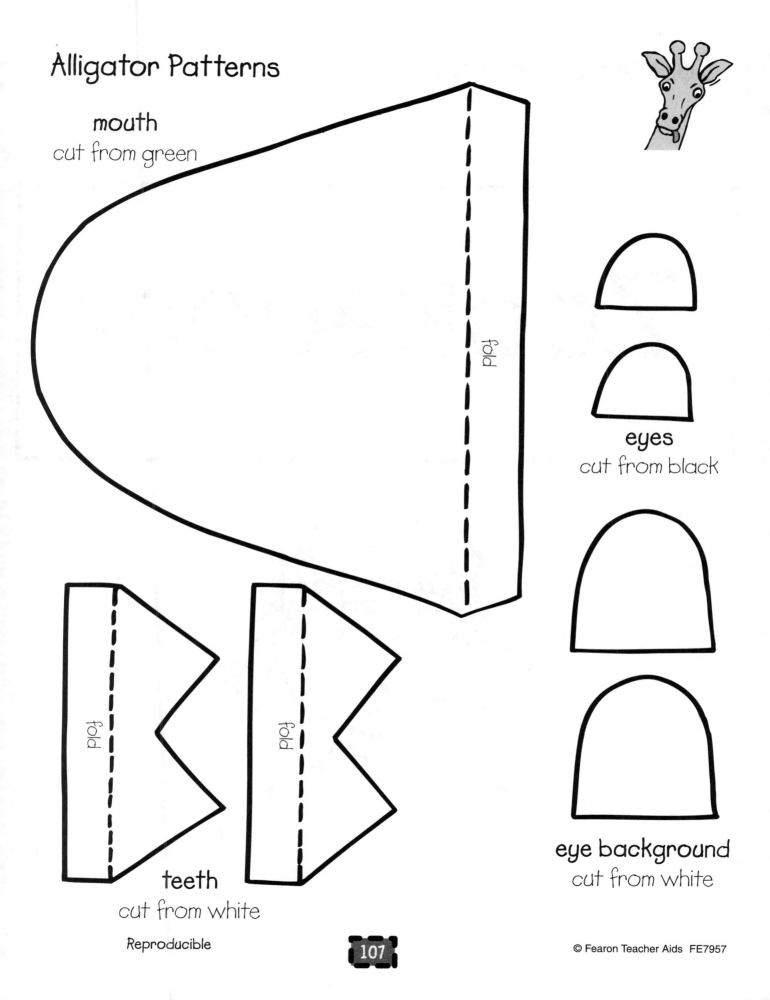

Zookeeper Hat Pattern

Zookeeper